MW01136790

Hermeneutics

Hermeneutics

Writings and Lectures, Volume 2

Paul Ricoeur

Translated by David Pellauer

polity

First published as *Écrits et conferences. 2. Herméneutique* © Editions du Seuil, 2010

This English edition © Polity Press, 2013

Polity Press
65 Bridge Street
Cambridge CB2 1UR, UK

Polity Press
350 Main Street
Malden, MA 02148, USA

All rights reserved. Except for the quotation of short passages for the purpose of criticism and review, no part of this publication may be reproduced, stored in a retrieval system, or transmitted, in any form or by any means, electronic, mechanical, photocopying, recording or otherwise, without the prior permission of the publisher.

ISBN-13: 978-0-7456-6121-6 (hardback)
ISBN-13: 978-0-7456-6122-3 (paperback)

A catalogue record for this book is available from the British Library.

Typeset in 11 on 13 pt Sabon
by Toppan Best-set Premedia Limited
Printed and bound in Great Britain by the MPG Books Group

The publisher has used its best endeavors to ensure that the URLs for external websites referred to in this book are correct and active at the time of going to press. However, the publisher has no responsibility for the websites and can make no guarantee that a site will remain live or that the content is or will remain appropriate.

Every effort has been made to trace all copyright holders, but if any have been inadvertently overlooked the publisher will be pleased to include any necessary credits in any subsequent reprint or edition.

For further information on Polity, visit our website: www.politybooks.com

Contents

Acknowledgments

The publishers gratefully acknowledge the following publications for permission to reproduce translations of some of the chapters:

"Metaphor and the Central Problem of Hermeneutics" was originally published in *New Literary History* 6 (1974): 95–110; and *Graduate Faculty Philosophy Journal* 3 (1973–4): 42–58.

"Towards a Hermeneutic of the Idea of Revelation" was published in *Harvard Theological Review* 70 (1977): 1–37.

Preface

Hermeneutics in the Work of Ricoeur

Hermeneutics, in France as elsewhere abroad, is frequently associated with the work of Paul Ricoeur. He contributed in many ways to making known this discipline devoted to the theory of interpretation, notably through two of his important collections of essays, *The Conflict of Interpretations* and *From Text to Action*, both of which bear the subtitle: *Essays in Hermeneutics*.[1] His own work is hermeneutic in two ways.

First of all, for Ricoeur hermeneutics constituted a philosophical *method*, one among others that he sought to articulate. This is particularly evident in his *Philosophy of the Will* volumes where Ricoeur integrates hermeneutics with a type of phenomenological analysis.[2] In these volumes Ricoeur seeks to provide a

---

[1] Paul Ricoeur, *The Conflict of Interpretations: Essays in Hermeneutics* (Evanston: Northwestern University Press, 1974); *From Text to Action: Essays in Hermeneutics II*, trans. Kathleen Blamey and John B. Thompson (Evanston: Northwestern University Press, 1991).

[2] Paul Ricoeur, *Freedom and Nature: The Voluntary and the Involuntary*, trans. Erzaim V. Kohák (Evanston: Northwestern University Press, 1966); *Fallible Man*, rev. trans. Charles A. Kelbley (New York: Fordham University Press, 1986); *The Symbolism of Evil*, trans. Emerson Buchanan (New York: Harper and Row, 1967).

phenomenological description of the voluntary in relation to the
involuntary, then, turning to confront the problem of an evil will,
he proposes an interpretation of the symbols of evil as they come
from the biblical tradition and that of Greek tragedy. Only such
an *interpretation* allows us to grasp the passage from the mere
possibility of erring (fallibility) to acknowledging the existence of
the fault. Then, to conclude, Ricoeur theorizes about the necessity
to articulate pure reflection on the basis of such linguistic symbols
which always precede it. This is the meaning of his well-known
aphorism, "the symbol gives rise to thought," which has to be
understood as a wager.[3]

More recently, in *Memory, History, Forgetting*, Ricoeur brings
together in a similar manner the phenomenology of memory and
a hermeneutic reflection bearing on our historical condition and
the explanatory understanding of human works.[4] These two
examples, among others, show that for him hermeneutics is a
philosophical method that cannot be set up as a universal method.
It can be used only where it turns out to be relevant, at the end
of a process of objectification and analysis, preliminary to reflections of a more ethical or ontological nature.[5] Hermeneutics thus
designates one of Ricoeur's ways of doing philosophy, in that he
is concerned – like Kant – to establish the conditions of validity
of different possible methods. The genius of hermeneutics, defined
as a "general theory of interpretation," is that it commits itself
scrupulously to the interpretation of human signs, whether they
be symbols, texts, or quasi-texts (actions).[6] As such, hermeneutics
presents itself as a distantiated, critical reflection on the operations of explanation and understanding at play in the interpretation of cultural artifacts, whether of an everyday or a more
scientific nature.

If, for Ricoeur, hermeneutics appears as a philosophical method
adapted to certain objects marked by their linguistic nature, it also

[3] *The Symbolism of Evil*, 347.
[4] Paul Ricoeur, *Memory, History, Forgetting*, trans. Kathleen Blamey and
David Pellauer (Chicago: University of Chicago Press, 2004).
[5] This is particularly clear in *Oneself as Another*, trans. Kathleen Blamey
(Chicago: University of Chicago Press, 1992), where the hermeneutic
moment constitutes a transition between an analytic description of
action and an ethics that itself leads to the sketch of an ontology.
[6] *From Text to Action*, xiii.

designates the very *style* of his philosophy insofar as it takes as its task coming to know the subject. As Ricoeur notes in his intellectual autobiography, this subject "does not know itself directly but only through the signs deposited in memory and in imagination by culture."[7] In this regard, the whole of Ricoeur's work bears the stamp of the "hermeneutical age of reason," to recall Jean Greisch's formula which Ricoeur applied to himself.[8] Hermeneutics is the face assumed by the philosophy of reflection when, in order to come to know the subject, philosophy chooses to take the long detour through the interpretation of signs of this subject's existence. In so doing, Ricoeur's philosophy illustrates a profound conviction: the way from the self to the self necessarily passes through the detour of what is other than the self. Or, to put it another way, the wish to know oneself will be premature if it does not take, in some way, the passage through the signs that speak about the world. In "On Interpretation," an essay from 1983 in which he looks back on and sums up the work he had done up until then, Ricoeur already presents hermeneutics as what completes and corrects his continued attachment to a philosophy of the subject, all too often forgetful of the mediations that any knowledge of the self presupposes (notably in Descartes but also in Husserl): "I should like to characterize this philosophical tradition by three features: it stands in the line of a *reflexive* philosophy; it remains within the sphere of Husserlian *phenomenology*; it strives to be a *hermeneutical* variation of this phenomenology."[9]

In the final analysis, it is because hermeneutics designates one method among others and also the style of his philosophy – that hermeneutics is the object of sustained, constant attention in his

[7] Paul Ricoeur, "Intellectual Autobiography," in Lewis Edwin Hahn, ed., *The Philosophy of Paul Ricoeur* (Chicago: Open Court, 1995), 16. The distinction between hermeneutic method and style is further developed in Daniel Frey, "Entre la méthod et le style: usages de l'herméneutique chez Ricoeur," in C. Sautereau and S. Catonguay, eds, *Usages de l'herméneutique* (Laval: Presses de l'université Laval, forthcoming).
[8] Jean Greisch, *L'Âge herméneutique de la raison* (Paris: Cerf, 1985). See also the Introduction to *Oneself as Another*, 25, and the title of the volume on Ricoeur from the *decade de Cerisy* dedicated to this thought: *Paul Ricoeur: Les Métamorphoses de la raison herméneutique*, ed. Jean Greisch and Richard Kearney (Paris: Cerf, 1991).
[9] *From Text to Action*, 12.

work – makes Ricoeur one of the leading thinkers in this tradition, alongside Schleiermacher, Dilthey, Heidegger, and Gadamer. The essays brought together in this second volume of "Essays and Lectures," published under the auspices of the *Fonds Ricoeur* (the Ricoeur Foundation), bear witness to this fact and to his contribution to hermeneutics.

Essays on Hermeneutics

Like the first volume in this series, this volume offers readers the opportunity to discover texts whose publication had been authorized by Paul Ricoeur, but which, because they originally appeared in works long out of print or in different languages, and which are not easily obtained, are still largely unknown, particularly to a French-speaking audience. Again, as with the first volume, the manuscripts of these texts, all reviewed by Ricoeur, are now held by the Ricoeur Archive. Hence it was not the desire to add a new volume on hermeneutics to a set of works now closed that motivated the editors of this volume, but rather a concern to offer a new entry to Ricoeur's important writings on interpretation. If his work on hermeneutics is in some ways better known abroad, notably in Italy and Germany, than in France, this was often because readers there had access to texts that, for all their being no less representative of Ricoeur's thinking, bear witness to his pedagogical concern to transmit clearly the main lines of his own contribution to modern hermeneutical theory.

This is the case for the set of four lectures brought together here under the title "The Hermeneutic Problem," which were delivered in Florence in May 1998 and published in an Italian translation following Ricoeur's death in 2005. These lectures gave Ricoeur the opportunity to condense the steps of his own development regarding hermeneutics. From the hermeneutics of symbols, which closed the *Freedom and Nature* volumes, through a hermeneutics centered on the "world of the text," to the elaborating of the ethical consequences of a hermeneutical theory of action, it is the unity of this development within a linguistic sphere that Ricoeur takes up and comments on for his listeners. Not only do these texts bear witness to the didactic concern of their author, they permit us to catch on the run, as it were, the advance in his research at the moment where the reflections were being elaborated that was to lead to the hermeneutics at work in his major work, *Oneself as Another*. Although these four lectures are sufficient unto themselves and can be read as such, they can equally serve as a guide for reading his major works.

Among the many articles devoted to hermeneutics that merit for one reason or another being discovered – or rediscovered – some, like "Metaphor and the Central Problem of Hermeneutics," which first appeared in 1972 in the *Revue Philosophique de Louvain*, marked important steps in the elaboration of Ricoeur's contribution to hermeneutical debates. Thus, one finds in this essay a condensed summary of the analyses devoted to metaphor and hermeneutics developed in *The Rule of Metaphor*, a condensation that is all the more valuable in that this essential text remains a difficult one owing to the technical nature of some of the discussions it presents (regarding Aristotle, Jakobson, Benveniste, Black, Frege, etc.).[10]

The lecture titled "Hermeneutical Logic?" first delivered in Paris at the Institut International de Philosophie in 1978, and then published in French in 1981, shows Ricoeur's knowledge of developments in hermeneutics, which was little known to his French audience; for example, that of Hans Lipps, from whom Ricoeur takes the title of his lecture. This lecture bears witness above all to Ricoeur's constant desire to confront the ontological hermeneutics inherited from Martin Heidegger and Hans-Georg Gadamer with the epistemological and logical questions raised by Jürgen Habermas and Karl-Otto Apel. A veritable "literature survey" of work dealing with hermeneutics since the 1960s, this text is an indispensable complement to the essays printed in *From Text to Action*, in which Ricoeur situated his own hermeneutical theory in relation to his predecessors (Heidegger and Gadamer). Like them, Ricoeur looks for a median position between ontological hermeneutics and the Habermasian critique of hermeneutics. This comes down to showing both sides that hermeneutics includes a critical dimension, one that assures it a real epistemological status.

---

[10] Paul Ricoeur, *The Rule of Metaphor: Multi-Disciplinary Studies in the Creation of Meaning in Language*, trans. Robert Czerny with Kathleen McLaughlin and John Costello, SJ (Toronto: University of Toronto Press, 1977).

This selection of Paul Ricoeur's texts devoted to hermeneutics would be incomplete if it silently passed by his insightful and, in the French context, rare, contribution to biblical hermeneutics. Thus it was necessary to include a couple of the essays that he designated (too modestly, no doubt) as his "intermittent incursions into the field of biblical exegesis" and "religious language."[11] Refusing the label of a Christian philosophy, preferring instead that of a "philosophy without any absolute," it was as a philosopher, not as a theologian, that Ricoeur looked at biblical literature (from both the Old and New Testaments), with the intention of asking how the Bible gives rise to thought.[12] "Hermeneutics of the Idea of Revelation," which dates from 1977, is without doubt one of his most influential essays on biblical hermeneutics. In it, Ricoeur proposes a dialectical understanding of the notions of revelation and truth that has important consequences. Besides this essay, which many people requested, are less typical essays, like the one – previously unpublished in French – included here titled "Salvation Myths and Contemporary Reason," which provides Ricoeur with the opportunity as a philosopher to consider the question of salvation by way of a reflection on myth and history.

Daniel Frey

[11] "Intellectual Autobiography," 41 and 24.
[12] Ibid., 13 and 53.

Editors' Note

The "essays and lectures" brought together in this book were chosen by Daniel Frey and Nicola Strickler, at the invitation of Catherine Goldenstein, administrator of the Ricoeur Foundation, Jean Greisch, and Jean-Louis Schlegel, all three members of the Editorial Committee of the Ricoeur Foundation. Daniel Frey and Nicola Strickler, as members of the Scholar's Advisory Committee of the Fonds Ricoeur, were responsible for the preparation of this edition and its annotations. As with the preceding volume, it is Ricoeur's complete texts as he left them that appear here. Any modifications have only to do with punctuation and the spelling of a few words, along with the corrections of some typographical errors. Ricoeur's own notes are indicated by the addition of the indication: Ricoeur's note. When the editors have added bio-graphical data to one of Ricoeur's own notes, this is indicated by the addition of the indication: ed. (= editors' addition).

D. F and N. S.

Translator's Note

The editors of the French edition of this collection of essays chose
to include numerous notes and annotations to these essays indi-
cating places in Ricoeur's and other authors' works where a topic
presented in them appears or is discussed. Their notes also
included explanations of some of the more technical terms, particularly those found in the essays that deal with biblical interpretation, that might not be familiar to all readers.

My working assumption in preparing this translation has been
that English-speaking readers would not be served by these references to French texts. Ricoeur's own notes, where they exist, and
references to any work he cites have, of course, been preserved,
and where English versions of the work in question are available
that is the title cited.

David Pellauer

Origin of the Texts

The Problem of Hermeneutics brings together four lectures presented to a seminar titled "Un itineratio filosifco: Seminario con Paul Ricoeur," offered at the Instituto Stensen in Florence from 19 to 22 May 1988. Ricoeur agreed at that time to allow the text to be translated into Italian and published, but it did not appear until after his death in an issue of *Filosfia e Teologia* 2 (2006): 236–73, devoted to his work.

Metaphor and the Central Problem of Hermeneutics was published in the *Revue philosophique de Louvain* 70 (1972): 93–115. Previous translations have appeared in English, German, Spanish, Polish, Japanese, and Norwegian.

"Hermeneutical Logic?" was presented as a lecture to the Institut international de philosophie in Paris in 1978. It was published in French in G. Fløistad, ed., *Contemporary Philosophy: A New Survey*, volume 1: *Philosophy of Language* (The Hague: Martinus Nijhoff, 1981), 179–223.

Hermeneutics of the Idea of Revelation is the text of a lecture given at the Facultés universitaires Saint-Louis in Brussels in 1976, later published in the volume Paul Ricoeur et al., *La Révelation* (Publications des Facultés universitaires Saint-Louis, 1977), 15–54, which includes the discussion that followed

Ricoeur's lecture, including questions from Edgar Haulotte and Emmanuel Levinas (207–36).

Salvation Myths and Reason first appeared in an Italian translation by E. De Dominicis, in G. Ferretti, ed., *La ragione e i simboli della salvezza oggi*, atti del quarto colloquio su filosofia et religion (Marcerata, 1988), Pubblicazioni della Facoltà di lettere e filosofia 53 (Marietti, 1990), 15–31. The French manuscript now is held in the Ricoeur Archive in Paris.

1

The Problem of Hermeneutics

I Hermeneutics and Symbolism

In this opening lecture I hope you will allow me to give an auto-biographical slant to my presentation and to speak of how for my own enlightenment I came upon the problems of symbolism.[1] This "historical" approach to my presentation seems to me to

[1] The four lectures presented here were given by Paul Ricoeur on the occasion of a seminar titled "Un itinerario filosofico: seminario con Paul Ricoeur," at the Instituto Stensen in Florence, Italy, held on May 19–21, 1988. They were published in an Italian translation under the title "I problemi dell'ermeneutica" in the journal *Filosofia e Teologia* 2 (2006): 236–73. In the French version of this text we kept the singular "herme-neutic" in conformity with the indication given by Ricoeur himself on the manuscript, even though the expression "The Problem of Herme-neutics" – inherited from Dilthey, Gadamer, and Bultmann – occurs frequently in his works. The first lecture "Hermeneutics and Symbol-ism" takes up in part the contents of another lecture given in 1987 on the occasion of an international symposium devoted to Ricoeur in Grenada, Spain, and published under the titled "Self-Understanding and History," in T. Calvo Martinez and R. Avila Crespo, eds, *Paul Ricoeur: Los caminos de la interpretación* (Barcelona: Anthropos, 1991), 9–25. Some elements of this lecture also appear in Ricoeur's "Intellectual Autobiography," in Lewis Edwin Hahn, ed., *The Philosophy of Paul Ricoeur* (Chicago: Open Court, 1995), 3–53.

have a certain didactic force, in that the breadth of the problem of interpretation appeared to me bit by bit, each time on the occasion of a particular and limited problem. Looking back, it seems to me that each of my books has been meant to answer a question with a well-delimited response that imposed itself on me. And the works that followed stemmed from those questions left unresolved by the preceding ones.

It was first of all along the trajectory of a philosophy of the will that the question of symbolism imposed itself for me in connection with one limited problem, that of the symbols of evil. This problem itself stemmed from the question left unresolved by a purely reflexive and eidetic analysis (in the Husserlian sense of these terms) of the structures of the voluntary and the involuntary.

If I chose to begin with the problem of the will, it was with the intention of giving a counterpart, in the practical order, to Merleau-Ponty's *Phenomenology of Perception*, which I admired unreservedly; I mean without the reservation that Merleau-Ponty himself was later to express in *The Visible and the Invisible*.[2] It seemed to me that what Merleau-Ponty had done for the theoretical field needed to be done for the practical one, namely, on the one hand, to give an eidetic analysis of the structures of the project, of voluntary motion, and of consent to the absolute involuntary, and, on the other hand, to give a dialectical analysis of the relations between activity and passivity. In seeking to provide a kind of complement to the *Phenomenology of Perception*, I also hoped to arbitrate for myself the confrontation between Husserl and Gabriel Marcel. To Husserl, I owed the methodology indicated by the term "eidetic analysis" (which is why I defined "decision" as the noesis whose noematic correlate was the project intended as "what was to be done"). But it was to Marcel that I owed the problematic of a subject both incarnate and capable of setting at a distance its desires and powers; in short, a subject master of itself, yet servant of that necessity figured by character, the unconscious, birth, and death. It was in order to respond to

[2] Maurice Merleau-Ponty, *Phenomenology of Perception*, trans. Colin Smith (London: Routledge and Kegan Paul, 1962); *The Visible and the Invisible*, ed. Claude Lefort, trans. Alphonso Lingis (Evanston: Northwestern University Press, 1968).

this twofold solicitation that I outlined an ontology equally opposed to monism and to dualism (that, for example, of Sartre in *Being and Nothingness*).[3] Using a language borrowed from Pascal, I spoke of an ontology of disproportionality.[4]

It was this ontology of disproportionality that I tried to elaborate for itself beyond *The Voluntary and the Involuntary* in *Fallible Man*.[5] I organized it in terms of three strong polarities and three corresponding fragile mediations. Thus, I saw the imagination, in the sense of the Kantian schematism, as mediating on the theoretical level between the finite perspective of perception and the infinite aim of the word. Similarly, on the practical level, respect bridged the finitude of character and the infinitude of happiness. Finally, the affective fragility characteristic of the passions of having, power, and worth seemed to me to come together in the amplitude of the feeling of belonging to the totality of things and the intimacy of being affected *hic et nunc*. One formula summed up this philosophical anthropology: *homo simplex in vitalitate, duplex in humanitate* (man is one as living, two as human).[6] In this way, the ontology of disproportionality underlying *Freedom and Nature* was made explicit. Monism and dualism were both set aside at the same time that reflective thought and the feeling which I called, with a Pascalian overtone, the "pathetique de la misère" were reconciled. These two works taken together illustrate what I believe to be my dominant concern, to integrate legitimate antagonisms and to make them bring about their own surpassing.

[3] Jean-Paul Sartre, *Being and Nothingness: An Essay on Phenomenological Ontology*, trans. Hazel Barnes (New York: Philosophical Library, 1956).

[4] See Blaise Pascal, *Pensées*, ed. and trans. Roger Ariew (Indianapolis: Hackett, 2005), 32–8.

[5] Paul Ricoeur, *Freedom and Nature: The Voluntary and the Involuntary*, trans. Erzaim V. Kohák (Evanston: Northwestern University Press, 1966); *Fallible Man*, rev. trans. Charles A. Kelbley (New York: Fordham University Press, 1986).

[6] In *Fallible Man*, Ricoeur attributes this formula to Maine de Biran (1766–1824), who in fact borrows it from Herman Boerhaave, *Praelectiones academicae de morbis nervorum* (Leyden: Jacob van Eems, 1761), 2:497. See also François Azouvi, *Maine de Biran: La Science de l'homme* (Paris: Vrin, 1995), 21n1; "Homo Duplex," *Gesnerus* 42 (1985): 229–44.

Yet, even broadened to become a fundamental anthropology, the philosophical position illustrated by *Freedom and Nature* remained fragmentary in the sense that it took into account only the formal structures of a will in general. What about the evil will, the "historical" figure of the will? Here is where phenomenology, even when enlarged to become an existential philosophy that can reconcile Husserl and Marcel, Mounier and Nabert (whom I had begun to discover and acknowledge), shows its limits. These are the same limits as those of the Cartesian *cogito*, with its ambition for immediacy, transparency, and apodicity. In order to get to the concrete evil will, it was necessary to introduce into the circle of reflection the long detour through symbols and myths, in short, the "historical" mediation of the cultural world. *The Symbolism of Evil* is what issued from this methodological shift.[7] There I say that the will recognizes itself as evil, and admits its guilt, only in meditating on the symbols and myths carried by the great cultural traditions that have instructed the Western mind, without speaking of other cultures that were not part of my finite memory.

Let me emphasize the personal side of this adventure. It was assuredly under the pressure of my two-sided cultural upbringing, both biblical and Greek, that I felt myself constrained to incorporate into the reflective philosophy coming from Descartes and Kant the interpretation of the symbols of stain, sin, and guilt, in which I saw the first symbolic layer of the consciousness of evil, followed by their interpretation in the great myths of the fall: the cosmogonic, orphic, tragic, and Adamic myths. In this way I was able to speak of a concrete reflection, owing to the lack of an ability to give the interpretation of these symbols and myths straight away the theoretical status indicated by the term hermeneutics. At this time, I was more focused on the continuity between the formal reflection practiced in *The Voluntary and the Involuntary* (1950) and the concrete reflection nourished by meditation on the symbols and myths about evil than on the break between hermeneutics and phenomenology. Moreover, at the time of *The Symbolism of Evil* (1960), it was the regional aspect of this symbolism, thematically circumscribed by the problem of the evil will,

[7] Paul Ricoeur, *The Symbolism of Evil*, trans. Emerson Buchanan (New York: Harper and Row, 1967).

that mattered most to me, rather than the universal aspect of symbolism.

Nevertheless, a first approximation of the hermeneutical problem could be drawn from this investigation limited to the symbolism of evil but bound to my more general definition of the symbol. I spoke of the symbol as any expression characterized by the phenomenon of having a double meaning, one where the literal signification indicates a second meaning which is accessible only through the reference of the first meaning to the second one. The latter condition is essential. The difference between a symbol and an allegory depends on it. In an allegory, the detour through a figurative expression has a purely didactic or ornamental function. It is always possible to say directly what has been said indirectly out of an intention to teach something or give pleasure. With the genuine symbol, the transfer from the literal to the figurative sense is the only means of access – this is what I showed for the domain of evil: stain is conveyed through the symbol of a spot, sin through that of a missed goal, guilt through the bite, the burden of a guilty conscience, etc.

That this double-meaning structure can be found elsewhere than in the symbolism of evil is what I expressed at the time through a "criteriology" of the symbol and the phrase "the symbol gives rise to thought." In this way, I already indicated the breadth and variety of the zones where a symbol could emerge: the cosmic aspect of hierophanies, the nocturnal one of oneiric productions, the creativity of poetic language. The first feature linked me to Eliade, the second to Freud and Jung, the third to Bachelard. In the end, it was to the latter that I was closest, particularly when he characterizes the poetic image as the expression of language born anew.

There was another expansion of my understanding of symbols beyond the particular example of the symbolism of evil. Already at that time, I proposed a general definition of myth as a symbol developed through a narrative, and articulated in terms of a time and space that could not be coordinated with those of history and geography using a critical method. For example, exile is a primary symbol of human alienation, but the story of the expulsion of Adam and Eve from Paradise is a second-order mythic narrative that makes use of characters, places, time, and amazing episodes. In a myth, a narrative plays the role of the literal meaning, but it is the transference toward a second meaning that makes myth belong to both the category of symbols and that of narrative.

Still, at this early stage of my investigations, hermeneutics had a limited definition that I had subsequently to enlarge. There is hermeneutics, that is interpretation, wherever there are expressions with a double meaning, where a second meaning gets unfolded starting from a first meaning. This definition is certainly a limiting one, but it does leave room for further development, thanks to the formula by which I ended *The Symbolism of Evil*: the symbol gives rise to thought. In saying this, I meant to emphasize both poles of the expression: the symbol "gives." Through its recourse to the archaic, the nocturnal, the oneiric, philosophy can escape the aporias connected to every attempt at a truly radical beginning for philosophy. A mediation on symbols starts from language that already exists and that has in some fashion already said everything. It comes down not to thought without any presuppositions, but to thinking starting from its presuppositions. What the symbol gives, gives rise to thought. This aphorism suggests that everything has already been said enigmatically, yet it is always necessary to start again when it comes to the dimension of concepts. "What is necessary," I said at that time, "is an interpretation that respects the original enigma of the symbols, that lets itself to be taught by them, but that, begining from there, promotes the meaning, forms the meaning in full responsibility of autonomous thought."[8] In 1960, however, I did not know how to articulate critical thought based on a repetition of myths and so I spoke vaguely of seeking "to go beyond criticism by means of criticism, by a criticism that is no longer reductive but restorative."[9] I called this a kind of post-critical, second naivety.

It was the double shock of psychoanalysis and structuralism that set me on the way to a critical hermeneutics and, in this way, called for a broader definition of hermeneutics than the deciphering of double-meaning expressions.

Here is how the hermeneutic problem became broadened under Freud's impact, as can be seen from the title of my book *Freud*

[8] *The Symbolism of Evil*, 349–50.
[9] Ibid., 350.

and Philosophy: An Essay on Interpretation.[10] The interpretation practiced in *The Symbolism of Evil* was spontaneously conceived of as an amplifying one, that is, an interpretation attentive to the surplus of meaning implicit in the symbolism of evil whose full sense only reflection could bring out. This amplifying interpretation, without saying anything about it or even knowing it, stood in opposition to a reductive interpretation which, in the case of guilt, seemed to me to be perfectly illustrated by Freudian psychoanalysis. A new type of polarity appeared to me, which announced what I was soon to call *The Conflict of Interpretations.*[11] Yet it was still within the limits of one determinate kind of symbolism that this conflict came to light. To be sure, the quasi integral reading of Freud's works that I undertook at that time quickly revealed to me that it came down to something quite other than a conflict limited just to the theme of guilt. What was at stake was, as Freud rightly saw, a philosophy of culture considered in its full breadth, wherein one found set forth the conflict between tradition and critical thought, just as had happened in the eighteenth century during the *Aufklärung*. My reading of the symbolism of evil was a traditional one, Freud's a critical one. My concern was not to sacrifice either one to the other, just as fifteen years earlier I had sought to conciliate Marcel and Husserl. The double reading of the Oedipus complex and myth that I propose, toward the end of my book on Freud, constitutes an appropriate illustration of the work of mediation raised by the conflict opened by psychoanalysis at the heart of my cultural tradition (which as I said earlier, was both biblical and Hellenic). I saw Freud as excavating an archeology of the cogito beneath the myth become a complex, an archeology that brought to light the archaic, infantile, neurotic aspects of sexuality, whereas Hegel – at least the Hegel of the *Phenomenology of Spirit* which I was then teaching at the Sorbonne – I saw as unfolding beyond the archaic figures of self-consciousness, a teleology of self-consciousness in which the truth of each figure was contained in the one that

[10] Paul Ricoeur, *Freud and Philosophy: An Essay on Interpretation*, trans. Denis Savage (New Haven: Yale University Press, 1970).
[11] Paul Ricoeur, *The Conflict of Interpretations: Essays in Hermeneutics*, ed. Don Ihde (Evanston: Northwestern University Press, 1974).

followed.[12] Was it not this same grafting of a teleology to an archeology of self-consciousness that Sophocles had in view when he drew a new tragedy of truth from an existing one of sexuality?

Whatever might be said about the theme of guilt, in terms of its precise limits, the question of a plurality and conflict of interpretation was opened. From the confrontation between Freud and tradition comes a conflict between two hermeneutics: an amplifying one, in the sense just referred to, and a hermeneutics of suspicion, wherein Freud stands alongside other teachers of suspicion, Feuerbach, Marx, and especially Nietzsche. In the new phase of my work that followed my work on Freud, my question no longer was limited to one particular set of symbols; it was open to the symbolic structure as a specific structure of language. This expansion of my project linked up with a change that had affected almost every school of philosophy, what has been designated as the linguistic turn.[13] Applied to the current in philosophy from which I came, this linguistic turn signified the passage from a phenomenology, even one broadened to become an existential phenomenology, to a hermeneutics with a focus on language.

This is where my conflict with structuralism played a decisive role in the broadening of the hermeneutical problem for me. What was at stake in this conflict? Nothing less than the fate of the question of the subject and of self-understanding. Whereas structuralism seemed to me to be a plea for an anonymous functioning, in the strongest sense of the term, of sign systems with no anchorage in subjectivity, the dimension of meaning seemed to me inseparable from the mediating role played by these systems with regard precisely to self-understanding. There could be no significance where a synchronic system of signs made no contribution to the diachrony, that is, the historicity of self-understanding. Here once again history – the history of signs in particular – was the obligatory mediation for any self-understanding.

The conflict between hermeneutics and structuralism is perhaps past today, at least in the form it took during the 1970s. What

[12] G. W. F. Hegel, *Phenomenology of Spirit*, trans. A. V. Miller (New York: Oxford University Press, 1977).
[13] See, e.g., Richard Rorty, ed., *The Linguistic Turn: Recent Essays in Philosophical Method* (Chicago: University of Chicago Press, 1967).

remains is the issue indicated by the title of my essay "Self-Understanding and History." The other topics, besides the dialectic of self-understanding and history taken up in my works from this period, all bear witness to this. I will only refer to one of them, because it will allow me to bring together several usually separated epistemological fields. I mean the dialectic of explanation and understanding. I devoted an essay to it now in *From Text to Action*.[14] The three epistemological fields I had in mind are the theory of the text, that of action, and that of history. In each of these fields the moment of understanding is characterized by an intuitive, overall insight into what is in question in this field, through an anticipation of meaning that touches on divination, marked by a commitment on the part of the knowing subject. The moment of explanation, on the other hand, is marked by the predominance of analysis, the subordination of a particular case to rules, laws, or structures, and by the setting at a distance of the object under study in relation to an independent subject. What was most important, to me, was not to separate understanding from explanation or vice versa, as was done, on the one side by the descendants of Romantic hermeneutics, and on the other, by the heirs of positivism. Interpretation, for me, consists precisely in the alternating of the phases of understanding and those of explanation along a unique "hermeneutical arc." Did I in this way get beyond the bit-by-bit character of my work of mediation? No, for I continue to think it is necessary to spell out in each case, in terms of the epistemological field under consideration, the particular style of alternation between explanation and understanding. In this regard, the respective domains of the text, action, and history have to be distinguished in terms of their specific constitutions.

In this triad, the notion of the text plays a central role. There, the old hypothesis that explanation reigns over the natural sciences and understanding over the so-called humanistic ones collapses. In fact, it was at the heart of these latter disciplines, more

[14] Paul Ricoeur, "Explanation and Understanding: On Some Remarkable Connections between the Theory of Texts, Action Theory, and the Theory of History," in *From Text to Action: Essays in Hermeneutics II*, trans. Kathleen Blamey and John B. Thompson (Evanston: Northwestern University Press, 1991), 125–43.

precisely in semiotics, that new models of explanation appeared that were exactly appropriate for the empire of signs; I mean ones of encoding and decoding. Because of this, it becomes more difficult to articulate explanation and understanding one in terms of the other, but it is also more difficult purely and simply to separate them. It seemed to me that a theory of discourse defined as the act by which someone says something about something to someone else could serve as the hinge that connected understanding and explanation. (Later, I shall speak of how my more recent reflections about rule-governed creation, about semantic innovation, as illustrated by metaphors, stem from this.)

As for the theory of action, which I was to return to in my subsequent work on narrative and also on ethics and politics, it illustrates the dialectic of explanation and understanding in the following way. The question is whether the language game containing terms like intention, motive, end, and so on has to be radically separated from the language game by which one speaks of movement, cause, event, and so on. There is a strong temptation to insist on a clear dichotomy between these two language games, which is a way of returning to the opposition between understanding and explanation. I try to show that, here again, the richer models of interpretation are the ones interweaving systematic and teleological segments within a complex phenomenon of intentional intervention in the course of the world, as we find in the model proposed by von Wright in a book titled precisely *Explanation and Understanding*.[15]

As for the theory of history, it presents in historical reasoning the most noteworthy illustration of the understanding of a framework of events organized in terms of a unique sequence and explanation in terms of generalities that in the most favorable cases take on the value of a law (as in demography, or economics). I discussed this in greater detail in the first volume of *Time and Narrative*.[16]

---

[15] G. H. von Wright, *Explanation and Understanding* (Ithaca: Cornell University Press, 1971).
[16] Paul Ricoeur, *Time and Narrative*, 3 vols, trans. Kathleen Blamey and David Pellauer (Chicago: University of Chicago Press, 1985–8).

I would sum up these three arguments by a single formula: to explain more is to understand better. In other words, if understanding precedes, accompanies, and envelops explanation, explanation in return analytically develops understanding.

I will end here this review of the successive extensions that my conception of hermeneutics underwent from *The Voluntary and the Involuntary* to the *Conflict of Interpretations*. As we have seen, my initial definition of hermeneutics as the unfolding of a second meaning, in double-meaning expressions of symbols, was not replaced but rather included in the dialectic of understanding and explanation. Later I shall speak of the new problems that gave rise to a further expansion, one marked principally by the notion of a "world of the text," of the hermeneutic problem, and what the result of this expansion was for the relation between phenomenology and hermeneutics which stood at the start of my reflective enterprise.

II Hermeneutics and the World of the Text

In this second lecture I want to take up again the development of the hermeneutical problematic at the point where I left it with the dialectic between explanation and understanding. You will recall that the notion of a text appeared as one of the "places" where this dialectic unfolds itself, along with the theory of action and that of history. At the end of this second lecture we shall see how history and action find themselves included within the theory of the text, precisely through the mediation of the notion of the world of the text which will be at the center of our investigation.

The Notion of the Text

A few words to begin about the notion of the text. Three comments:

(a) As I stated in my first lecture the notion of the text presupposes a conception of discourse that goes beyond than that of speech (*parole*) opposed to the system of language (*langue*) so

dear to Saussure (speech as use vs. system).[17] Discourse implies a
synthetic activity to which get grafted the diverse kinds of semantic innovation that I am going to talk about. Discourse articulates
a subject of discourse, an act of discourse, a content of discourse,
a meta-linguistic code, an extra-linguistic reference, and an inter-
locutor. This can be summed up by the formula: someone following common rules says something about something to someone
else. In other words, a "speaker," something "said," a "saying"
(or meaning), a "world" (or referent), rules (phonological, lexical,
and syntactical), and an "allocution."

(b) A second presupposition of the notion of a text has to do
with the distinction between the *oral* and *written* use of discourse.
Passing from speaking to writing indicates much more than a
simple fixation or inscription applied to a discourse that could
have been said orally. There really is writing when the produced
discourse was never spoken aloud and, in fact, could not have
been spoken aloud. Writing announces itself as the impossibility
of speaking aloud; a new instrument of thinking and of discourse
is born with writing.

First consequence: an alternative is opened that points the way
to what Jean Starobinski calls "the story of criticism." On the
one hand, the phenomenon of inscription gives a special authority
to what is written down. On the other hand, the distance thereby
established from speaking aloud engenders a suspicion – and a
question: how could such a meaningful effect have been produced? In a word, the conflict between *authority* and *genesis* is
inaugurated.

Second consequence: from the single fact that discourse is
written down, it has a history that is no longer that of its author.
This paradox is easy to understand. The meaning of what has
been written down is henceforth separate from the possible intentions of its author and hence removed from any kind of psychologizing critique. What we can call the *semantic autonomy* of the
text means that the text unfolds a history distinct from that of its
author. The ambiguity of the notion of signification reflects this
situation. To signify can mean what the text signifies or what the

[17] Ferdinand de Saussure, *Course in General Linguistics*, ed. Charles
Bally and Albert Sechehaye in collaboration with Albert Riedlinger,
trans. Wade Baskin (New York/London: McGraw-Hill 1966).

author meant to signify (in English: what does the text mean? What do you mean?). This disconnection between saying and signifying already constitutes a phenomenon of production, of creation.

Another consequence: oral discourse makes a place of a face-to-face relation, a dialogue in the proper sense of the term, such that it is always possible for the interlocutors to *point out* to each other the objects their conversation is about. This reference to things in the world is, as one says, *ostensive*. It is this ostensive reference that writing abolishes. If I read in a poem, "that night..." I understand that the deictic "that" in play here, as a demonstrative term, does not indicate anything one can point to. This kind of suspending of the deictic function with the text initiates a shift in relation to every kind of reality capable of being pointed to. It is in relation to this eclipsing of the ostensive reference that we shall pose in a moment the question whether *literature*, whether as lyric or narrative, can be said to *refer* to something that we can still call a "world" – the world of the text.

Last consequence linked to writing: the written text is addressed to another audience than the human face. The single fact that a text is open, in Gadamer's terms, to anyone who knows how to read implies that the author of oral discourse yields his or her place to an invisible reader and, at the limit, to an unlimited, undetermined audience.[18] Here is where the unknown adventure of the text begins.

(c) The third presupposition behind the idea of a *text*, which is common to both speech and writing, but developed by the text to an extreme degree, has to do with the *composition* (text also means *texture*) that makes the text into a work. Once an author undertakes to write something down, he or she undertakes to compose things in a way that differs from the exchange of words characteristic of the dialogical exchange. The semantic autonomy of writing which I have referred to opens the way to an investigation into the rules of composition that the rapid exchange of answers and questions in a conversation does not have the leisure to develop. The *work* has its specific rules of composition that

---

[18] Hans-George Gadamer, *Truth and Method*, second, rev. edn, rev. trans. Joel Weinsheimer and Donald G. Marshall (New York: Crossroad, 1991), 392.

make it a narrative, a poem, an essay, and so on. And this problem of composition does not come from linguistics for which the last unit considered is the *sentence*, but from poetics, which has to do precisely with the modes of composition for a discourse, most often (but not necessarily) one that is written down, whose units are longer than a sentence. This phenomenon of having a texture, of being a composition, opens a series of new alternatives, no longer that between authority and genesis, but rather between the consistency of a text as a tightly structured thing and its opening to the sides of the world and the reader. It is the problem of a dialectic of sense and reference, on one side, and of writing and reading, on the other. We are going to see how these two problems are closely connected.

The World of the Text

In *The Rule of Metaphor* and *Time and Narrative* I worked out this notion of the world of the text, by extending my reflection on the referential function of *non-descriptive* discourses, such as poems and narratives.[19] Literature, in my opinion, brings to light a major enigma having to do with language, namely, the battle within it between two diverging orientations that are already present in ordinary language, but which do not become manifest except at the level of those large-scale units of composition that make up texts and works. On the one side, language seems to exile itself from the world, closing itself in on its structuring and functioning and finally celebrating itself in glorious solitude. The *literary* status of language illustrates this first orientation. On the other side, contrary to this centripetal tendency, literary language seems capable of augmenting its power to discover and transform reality – especially human reality – by taking a distance on the descriptive function of the ordinary language of conversations. In truth, this double pulsation can be caught sight of by means of a

[19] Paul Ricoeur, *The Rule of Metaphor: Multi-Disciplinary Studies in the Creation of Meaning in Language*, trans. Robert Czerny with Kathleen McLaughlin and John Costello, SJ (Toronto: University of Toronto Press, 1977); *Time and Narrative*, 3 vols, trans. Kathleen Blamey and David Pellauer (Chicago: University of Chicago Press, 1985–8).

simple reflection on the relation between signs and things. In that the sign is not the thing, it indicates the possibility of exile. Yet there is not a world of signs. The sign rather is about the world. In ordinary language, this double pulsation – out of the world, toward the world – takes place with no problem. Reference always compensates for the distance meaning assumes. This is the principle behind the functioning of all directly descriptive discourse. But it is different with *literature*, with the inventiveness of literary language. There, discourse is in a way reinforced and consolidated in its exile through the very activity of composition that gives a text an autonomous existence; one might even say a power of subsistence outside the world. Then it is in the encounter with this glorious exile that the opposite impulse occurs, which, in an apt expression of Gustave Guillaume, "turns language back toward the universe."

It was this problem of the return of the sign toward the thing at the level of the metaphorical statement that was at issue in *The Rule of Metaphor* and *Time and Narrative*.

Where does the difficulty come from? It comes from the fact that in poetry as in the fictional narrative the *semantic innovation* seems to eclipse any *reference to the world*, to the point of rendering it superfluous, if not incongruous, impertinent. In both cases, the production of a new meaning is bound to synthetic operations that create new forms of discourse. In the case of metaphor, it is the unheard of comparison between two incompatible semantic fields following the usual rules of classification that creates the spark of meaning constitutive of the live metaphor. In the well-known verse by Charles Baudelaire: "Nature is a temple where living columns…" no word taken for itself (nature, temple,…) is metaphorical, but it is the comparison with "living columns" that forces one to *see* life *as* architecture and architecture *as* life.[20]

The theory of narrative brings a comparable phenomenon to light: The plot of a narrative is also a synthesis of the heterogeneous in that by bringing together the facts recounted into one told story it draws a unified narrative from the dust cloud of

---

[20] Charles Baudelaire, "Correspondances," in *Les Fleurs du mal*, iv, ed. A. Adam (Paris: Garnier, 1961), 13; *The Flowers of Evil*, trans. Keith Waldrop (Middleton, CT: Wesleyan University Press, 2007), 14.

events, where in doing this the plot combines intentions, causes, and accidents, and in the end pulls together a temporal configuration from a succession of discrete events. The configuring act of the plot thereby becomes symmetrical to what I have called the "odd" predication found in metaphor.

It was from this analysis of the semantic innovation at work in poetic discourse, thanks to metaphor, and in narrative discourse, on the basis of the plot, that I based my reflections on the *world of the text*. This counterpart to semantic innovation is at its peak in poetry and the narrative art. It is the power of *opening* language further to the world, as though the creativity found in language at the same time were to express a *surplus* of referentiality.

Let me recall briefly, with an eye to further discussion, how I approached this difficult and controversial problem of reference, first of all in *The Rule of Metaphor*, then in *Time and Narrative*.

In the chapter in *The Rule of Metaphor* titled "Metaphorical Reference," I strongly uphold the thesis that the suspending of a first-degree reference, that of discourse in its descriptive functioning, was just the other side of an infinitely more remarkable process, which I characterize as a redescription of the world, comparable to the role of models in scientific knowledge. Today I readily admit that this miracle of a metaphorical reference leaves unanswered the question of whether it is language itself that refers, or the one who states it; and therefore the question arises of knowing under what conditions someone speaking metaphorically refers obliquely to the world.

It was at this stage of perplexity and ambiguity that *Time and Narrative* takes up the problem of reference within the framework of a literary use of language. It does so, I believe, with better chances of success. The problem has become that of the passage from the configuration within the narrative text to the refiguration of the real world of the reader outside the narrative text. This problematic gets its *lettres de noblesse* from Aristotle's *Poetics* which assigns to *muthos* – the plot – a *mimetic* function with regard to the world of action, of *praxis*. Narrative language is therefore not locked in on itself since it refers to the action of human beings following a relation that has no equivalent – mimesis – which is not one of a mere imitation, in the sense of a copy, a replica, a reduplication, but rather one of a reorganization at a higher level of significance and efficacity. The overly simple thesis about a power of redescription assigned to the metaphorical utterance as such finds itself enriched by the addition of multiple mediations that assure the transition between the configuration in the narrative and the refiguration of the world of praxis. These multiple mediations are outlined in the first volume [of *Time and Narrative*] under the heading of a threefold mimesis: prefiguration, configuration, refiguration. I shall not speak of them here in order to be able to devote a few lines to the detailed analyses that were meant to unfold this initial sketch of what was at issue.

Broadly speaking, I see three stages along the road from configuration to refiguration. At the end of volume 2 [of *Time and Narrative*], I first develop the idea that a literary text in general, a narrative one in particular, projects before itself a *world-of-the-text*, a possible world, to be sure, but a world nevertheless, a place I can think of myself inhabiting in order to carry out there my own-most possibilities. Without being a real world, this intentional object intended by the text as its outside-the-text constitutes a first mediation, inasmuch as what a reader can appropriate is not the lost intention of the author behind the text, but the world of the text in front of the text. The second stage along this route is the refiguration constituted by my long investigation devoted to the aporias of the experience of time. How are they of interest to our problem? In that the narrative text finds standing over against it not simply everyday practices, but another discourse, one that engenders our perplexities concerning human time. Without a narrative articulation, in effect, our experience of time is prey to insoluble paradoxes for purely speculative thought. One needs only to think of the disproportion between the brief time of mortals and the long time of the movement of the stars. But this disproportion is not only quantitative, it is qualitative for a time with a past, present, and future – in other words, for a time of attention, anticipation, and memory – and a time without a present, constituted by an infinite series of instants that are merely virtual cuts in the continuity of changes. This aporetics of time, as I refer to it, constitutes to my eyes the major transition between the configuration internal to narrative and the refiguration of action brought about by narrative. I see narrative activity as the "poetic" reply to this aporetics of time. Not that narrative as told resolves the paradoxes of time. But at least it renders them productive. This is why the term a poetics of narrative gets placed over against the aporetics of time. In this way, narrative "imitates" action, by offering a narrative articulation to an experience of time that without it would remain handed over to the endless paradoxes that run the risk of turning philosophy into sophistry. The third stage in the direction of the refiguration of the practical field by narrative is constituted by the *act of reading*. This was the missing link in the chapter on metaphorical reference in *The Rule of Metaphor*. Who or what refers?, we asked a little while ago. It is the reader. The real character who brings about the intersection of the (possible) world of the text with the (real) world of the reader. At the end of my itinerary I propose a theory of reading where two strategies clash: that of the author, under the mask of the narrator, and that of the reader. The former is a strategy of persuasion exercised by the narrator and directed toward the reader, thanks to the "willing suspension of disbelief" (Coleridge) that characterizes the entry into reading.[21] The second is the strategy of a game, even of a battle, involving suspicion and rejection, that allows the reader to practice the distance of appropriation

III Semantics of Action and of the Agent

In this third lecture I want to present a schematic idea of the theory of action upon which I shall base my comments on the ethics of action in my concluding lecture.

What I will propose here is a "semantics of action," in which I sum up my analyses published under the title "The Discourse of Action," to which I shall next add some new developments regarding the relation between the agent and his or her action, so as to complete an analysis of the *what* and *why* of action by an analysis of its *who*.[22] It is this latter question that will bring us next time to my reflections on ethics.

We must first delimit what we mean by semantics, as it is defined by analytic philosophy, in relation to a pragmatics of

[21] Samuel Taylor Coleridge, *Biographia Literaria*, The Collected Works, vol. 7, ed. J. Engell and W. Jackson Bate (Princeton: Princeton University Press, 1983): 2:6.
[22] See Paul Ricoeur, "Le discours de l'action," in Dorian Tiffeneau, ed., *La Sémantique de l'action* (Paris: CNRS, 1977), 1–137.

language. For semantics, the principal accent is placed, for one thing, on the meaning of propositions independently of any positing of subjects of their utterance; for another, on the reference to entities external to language. Hence semantics seeks to answer two questions: *what* does one say? *About what* is it said? As for pragmatics, it focuses on propositions whose meaning depends on the usage each speaker makes of them, consequently on the positing of this speaker and his or her singular perspective on the world. We can already say that the semantics of action can suffice to designate action as a kind of event one can talk about, but it is not sufficient, by itself, to designate the agent as capable of designating him- or herself as this agent.

The Conceptual Scheme of Action

The most noteworthy insight of the semantics of action for practical philosophy is that it orients our gaze to an analysis of the *conceptual scheme* in which we find inscribed all those notions that, in ordinary language, apply to human action. This conceptual scheme contains notions such as circumstances, intentions, motives, deliberation, voluntary or involuntary motion, passivity, constraint, intended or unintended results, and so forth. The open-ended character of this list is less important here than its organization as a *network*. What counts for making sense of each one of these terms is that it belongs to the same network as do all the others. Hence relations of intersignification govern their meanings, such that knowing how to make use of one of them is knowing how to make use of the whole network in a meaningful and appropriate way. This amounts to a coherent language game, in which the constitutive rules that govern the use of one term make up a system with those that govern the use of another term. This conceptual network must not be taken to be a simple list of idiomatic expressions belonging to some language, English for example. It has to be taken as the transcendental condition for any discourse about action. Unlike with empirical concepts, the whole network functions to determine what "counts as" action in the psychological and social sciences that study behavior. An effective way of proceeding to this mutual determination of notions belonging to one and the same network is to identify the chain of questions capable of being posed about the subject of any action: who does or did what, in view of what, how, in what circumstances, with what means and what results? The key notions in this network draw their meaning from their specific nature as answers that can be given to these specific questions which, themselves, are meaningful in terms of one another: who, what, why, how?

What needs to be shown is that the question "who?", which appears here for the first time as a distinct question in comparison to the question "what?", is nonetheless incorporated into the whole network of questions governing the interrelated meanings that make up the language game of action. The *who* of action – the agent – remains tributary to the question *what*, having to do with the action itself as one variety of event in the world. It is only through the detour of attributing the action predicates to a logical subject of the verbs of action that the agent as agent is distinguished from the action. But, even then, the question *who* remains in a way, in a semantics of action, a variant of the question *what*, inasmuch as the agent is one of the "things" about which we speak.

Let us continue to follow the movement by which the semantics of action brings us to the threshold of the question *who* through the detour of the questions of *what* and *why*.

The What of Action

The question *what* can be asked regarding those verbal predicates characteristic of action sentences; for example: "to do something." These verbal predicates pose interesting philosophical problems to which analytic philosophy has devoted highly precise analyses. At the center of these discussions is the relation between an action and an event. At first, one emphasized the "logical gap" that separates these two notions. An action, one noted, is not something that simply happens, like an event that just occurs, but something that is made to happen.[23] The argument then goes like

---

[23] For a detailed presentation of this argument, see A. I. Melden, *Free Action* (London: Routledge and Kegan Paul, 1961); Stuart Hampshire, *Thought and Action* (Notre Dame, IN: University of Notre Dame Press, 1983). – Ricoeur's note.

this: what happens is the object of an observation, hence of a constative statement that is either true or false. What one makes happen is not true or false, but it does make true or false an assertion about a certain occurrence.

I would connect to the same argument the distinction G. E. M. Anscombe draws between knowing-that and knowing-how.[24] This notion applies to events "known without observation," which links up with the "practical knowledge" that interests us here. This notion of events "known without observation" is relevant to our discussion in that it points in the same direction as the opposition just referred to between assertions verified by the physical sciences and statements that action makes true. For example, I know without observation my actions done intentionally, which I will say more about in a moment, but also the position of my body and my limbs, and still more the motives that make me act in a certain way, about which we say that they "push" us to act in this or that way. All this comes down to knowing-how, not knowing-that. The meaning of a gesture is in the gesturing: "*his* knowledge of what is done is practical knowledge"; "a man has practical knowledge who knows how to do things."[25]

The Why of Action

We draw closer to the question *who* in passing from the question *what* to the question *why*. A new opposition gets proposed that indicates the specificity of the conceptual network of action and the language game about action.

It is with the opposition between "motive" and "cause" that the logical gulf appears to be deepest. A motive – it was noted – is always a "motive for" or a "motive to." As such, it is logically implied in the notion of "action," in the sense that we cannot mention the motive without mentioning the action for which it is the motive. The notion of cause, at least in the Humean sense (for nothing says that this sense exhausts the semantic field

[24] G. E. M. Anscombe, *Intention* (Oxford: Basil Blackwell, 1957; Cambridge, MA: Harvard University Press, 2000).
[25] Ibid., 82, 88.

of causes, as I shall say later on), implies a logical heterogeneity between a cause and its effect, inasmuch as I can mention the one without mentioning the other – for example, the match without the fire. The intimate, logical connection characteristic of motivation is exclusive of the extrinsic, contingent connection of causality. The argument claims to be logical, not psychological, in the sense that it is the logical force of the motivational connection that excludes our classifying motives as causes. Motives are better interpreted as "reasons for..."

I would like to say something about how I situate myself in this discussion. The thesis about the duality of two universes of discourse, whose development we have been following from the opposition between happening and making happen up to the opposition between a cause and a motive, seems to me to draw an erroneous conclusion from analyses that are partly correct. The correctness of the analysis has to do with the irreducibility of psychic predicates to physical ones attributed to the agent of an action – I shall come back to this later with the help of Peter Strawson's book *Individuals*.[26] The false conclusion is the disjunction between two universes of discourse, one psychic, the other physical. An action is at the same time a certain configuration of physical movements and an accomplishment able to be interpreted in terms of intentions and motives. These two language games are not juxtaposed but rather superimposed. The semantics of action here adds a mixed category, that of *desire*, which requires conjoining psychic categories, exclusively reserved for persons, with physical categories that belong both to persons and things. The relevance of this mixed category was overlooked in the earlier analysis of motives, in that it was placed on the side of "reasons for," hence of rational justification. In this way, one hid what is odd about desire, namely, that it has a *meaning* that can be spoken of using the language of intentions, and as a *force* using the language of physical energy.

I see three typical contexts in which motives are effectively experienced as a cause in the sense of what moves one to do something. The first context is the one where to the question "what led you to do that?" one gives an answer that states neither

[26] Peter Strawson, *Individuals: An Essay in Descriptive Metaphysics* (London: Methuen, 1959).

an antecedent, in the Humean sense of a cause, nor a reason, in the sense of a rationale, but rather a sudden impulse or, as one says in psychoanalysis, a drive (in German, a *Treib*, in French, *une pulsion*). Second context: the one where, to the slightly different type of question, "why do you habitually do such things?", the answer mentions a disposition, an enduring, even a permanent tendency. Third context: if to the question "what made you (involuntarily) jump?" you respond, "a dog frightened me," you do not join, as in the preceding cases, the *how* to the *what*, but the object to its cause. This last context is characteristic of *emotion*. The specific feature of emotions, from the point of view of their linguistic expression, is that object and cause stand in a reciprocal relation. These three contexts can be brought together under the general heading of affections or passions in the old sense of the term. In these three contexts, a certain passivity appears correlative to the action of doing something.

This passivity means that the relation between desiring and doing cannot be reduced to the justification that a purely rational agent gives to his action. Such an action would precisely be one done without desire. This phenomenology of desire, extended to include being affected, forces us to say that, even in the case of rational motivation, motives would not be motives for action unless they were also causes.

To be sure, admitting this requires reworking the notion of a cause, in parallel with that of a motive, irreducible to a "reason for." The prestige of the Humean model (of a causal antecedent with no logical connection to the result) has prevented philosophers from recognizing the cases where motive and cause are indiscernible, that is, all those cases that express the old idea of an efficient cause or disposition, which the Galilean revolution pushed out of physics, but which need precisely to be integrated into their land of origin, our experience of desire.

We still need to complete the movement that, from the question "what?" (what action?), leads, by way of the question "why?" (with what intention, for what motive?), toward the question "who?" (what agent?).

In the preceding remarks, we have remained, for purely didactic reasons, with the limits of a semantics of action without an agent. This semantics could be developed to a great extent insofar as action appears in the world as something about which one can speak. We were able initially to extend this semantics of action to intentions and motives, inasmuch as these describe or explain action. However, intentions and motives also apply to the side of the agent of action, inasmuch as they are *his*. A notion of "belonging-to" appears here that forces us to pass from the action to its agent.

Semantics of Ascription

The relation of an action to its agent is the type of problem I spoke of in my opening remarks as being both old and new. That action depends on its agent, in a specific sense of the relation of dependency, had been indicated by Aristotle, well before the Stoics, without his, for all that, really being able to deal with this relation in a thematic way. The language of his analysis, in Book III of the *Nichomachean Ethics*, points to a kind of wisdom whose depths he was unable to fathom. It is true that this language is not handed over to chance. Aristotle was certainly one of the first, after the Sophists, perhaps, to verify and codify the relevance of the linguistic choices made by the orators, the tragic dramatists, the magistrates, and ordinary language itself, as soon as it is a question of submitting action and its agent to a moral judgment. This is why the care Aristotle takes in making distinctions and offering definitions merits our examining them from the point of view of the language resources they make use of.

An old problem, the ascription that connects action to its agent has become a new problem, owing to the refining of the theory of predication in general and the semantics of action in particular.

I would like to show that the semantics of action leads to giving "ascription" a distinct signification that transforms particular cases into exceptions and sets us on the way to the question of the identity of the self.[27]

Strawson, the author of *Individuals*, observes that physical and mental characteristics *belong* to the person, that the latter *possesses* them. What an "owner" can dispose of is said to be his "own" in contrast to what belongs to someone else and which,

---

[27] The remainder of this section is drawn from Ricoeur's *Oneself as Another*, 94–6.

owing to this fact, is said to be foreign to him. In turn, this "ownness" governs the meaning that we give to those adjectives and pronouns that we speak of precisely as "possessives": "my/ mine," "your/yours," "his/hers." Nor should we overlook the impersonal form, "to each his own," an expression I shall return to in the next lecture.[28]

The question is whether these expressions, which are often idiomatic, rest on universal meanings that merit being assimilated to the transcendental terms for the semantic field in question. There is good reason to think this is so. It is remarkable, for example, that ascription makes all the terms in the conceptual network of action pivot around the question "who?"; conversely, we determine the answer to the question *who* by procuring an answer to the chain of questions *what*, *why*, *how*, and so on. Let us verify this for the question *what* and the question *why*.

It is of action itself that we first say it is my action, your action, his action, that it depends on someone and is in his or her power. It is similarly in regard to intentions that we say that it is some-one's intention and that, regarding someone, we say that he or she "intends to..." We can certainly understand an intention as an intention. But if we detach it from its author to examine it, we restore it to the person in question as being his or her own. This, moreover, is what the agent him- or herself does when he or she considers the options open to him or her and deliberates on them, according to Aristotle. Ascription consists precisely in the agent's reappropriation of his or her own deliberations and preferences. To decide, to make up one's mind, is to cut off the discussion by making one's own one of the contemplated options. As for the notion of a motive, insofar as it is distinguished from that of an intention – for example, in the case of what Anscombe calls "backward-looking motives" – its belonging to an agent is as much a part of its meaning as is its logical tie to the action itself for which it is the cause. We can legitimately ask: "Why did A do X?" "What led A to do X?" To mention the motive is also to mention the agent. There is something particularly strange, paradoxical, involved here.

On the one hand, the search for the author is a terminable inquiry that ends with the determining of the agent, generally

---

[28] In fact, the next lecture makes no mention of the "impersonal."

designated by a proper name. "Who did this? So and so." On the other hand, the search for motives for an action is interminable, the chain of motivations losing itself in the impenetrable fog of internal and external influences. Psychoanalysis stands in direct relation to this situation. But this does not mean that we cannot tie the interminable search for motives to the terminable one for an agent. It is this odd relation that is part of our concept of ascription. Therefore it is as a function of the whole network that makes up the semantics of action that we make sense of the expression: *agent*. This remark is an occasion to recall that mastery of this whole network is comparable to learning a language and that understanding the word "agent" is learning how to place it correctly in this network.

Ascription and the Ability to Act

Having said this, is it possible to be more precise regarding the relation of ascription in another way than through this back-and-forth play of the terms of a conceptual network that governs the semantics of action? This greater precision, which is still lacking, stems in my opinion from analyses that go beyond the framework of the semantics of action. What still remains in suspense is the very notion of being able to do something or of "agency," which bridges agent and action. But what do we mean by agency? Must we limit ourselves to the two Aristotelian metaphors of paternity and ownership?

I see two directions in which the analysis of agency might be pursued. Following the first direction, if the ascription by which an action is attributed to an agent differs logically from mere attribution, this is owing to its kinship with moral and juridical imputation, about which I shall speak further in a little while.

The intention that presides over this assimilation of agency and moral and juridical imputation is legitimate. It tends to fill in the gap that separates ascription in the moral sense and attribution in the logical sense. This gap also applies to the meanings assigned to the terms "possess" and "belongs to," when they relate to agency. The agent, we may say, is the owner of his actions which thereby belong to him. It belongs to someone, we also say, to do this or that.

But we can doubt whether moral or juridical imputation constitutes the strongest form of a logical structure for which agency would be a weaker version, and this is so for several reasons.[29] First reason: Juridical utterances seem to apply only selectively to actions considered from the angle of whether they are blamable or punishable. Blameable act are ones judged to be wrong through a verdict that condemns them. Second reason: the imposition of an accusation – a verdictive – on the simple ascription of an action to an agent presupposes that one has already formed the idea of an agent capable of designating him- or herself as the cause of his or her acts. But this self-designation does not necessarily have a moral or juridical coloration. It stems simply – as I shall show in my next lecture – from a theory of speech-acts that implies references to a speaker. Final reason: far from the assigning of responsibility in an ethico-juridical sense providing the decisive criterion of ascription, it presupposes a causal sense of agency that has yet to be determined. Action has to be able to be spoken of as depending on an agent if it is to fall under the headings of blame and praise. Thus, in his *Nichomachean Ethics*, Aristotle prefaced his theory of virtues, as we have already noted, with an analysis of a basic act, preference, through which is expressed a form of agency more primitive than the blameworthy or praise-worthy character – today we would say that it is "judgeable" – of the action produced.

So we have to turn to our second type of analysis of agency, centered on it causal efficacy. Specific difficulties await us on this second path.

First difficulty: treating agency as a kind of non-Humean causality means reentering the field of Kantian antinomies concerning causality. Earlier we distinguished between the terminable character of causality applied to an agent and its interminable character when applied to motives. In one case, the inquiry ends with a proper name, in the other it gets lost in an endless search. So the agent turns out to be a strange cause since he or she puts an end to the search for a cause. In this way, the agent finds him- or herself placed on the side of the thesis about finitude in the Kantian antinomy, the thesis that it is necessary to stop at a first

[29] The remainder of this paragraph is drawn from *Oneself as Another*, 100–1.

term in the series of causes, whereas the motive falls on the side of the antithesis, which is infinite because it excludes our assigning a beginning to any causal series.

The only riposte to this first difficulty is to reject the Humean presupposition in order to return to a concept of causality appropriate to the production of an action by its agent. Will someone condemn the anthropomorphism of this conception of production, which we could well call Aristotelian? If that were the case, it would be plausible to reply that the semantics of action points the concept of causality back toward its birth place, namely, human action: the *aitia*, or cause, becomes once again indiscernible from its *aition*, its responsible agent.

Here a new difficulty arises. It has to do with the primitive character of agency taken in the sense of causal agency. To put it briefly, in every case, is not alleging a primitive relation to run the risk of an overly lazy argument, one whose tautological character is easily unmasked? We can call the relation of action to its agent causal, but only on the condition that "to cause" means "to produce" in the sense of causal efficacy.

There is a reply to this objection, it seems to me. In order to escape the charge of circularity, one can turn to a style of transcendental argument meant to show that the notion of causal efficiency, of causal agency, is the condition of possibility of certain effective procedures by which, over the course of an action, we try to disentangle what, in the final analysis, depends on the agent, on some agent.

We must first of all dissociate, in actions that produce changes in the world (displacements, manipulations, transformations), what is a more or less distant *effect* of the action, and which can be called its result, from the initial, simple physical impulse. This is not just the most frequent case, but the most typical one when we speak of acting, that is, precisely, *causing* changes in the world. Any attribution to an agent is a problem inasmuch as this agent is no longer present in the long-term consequences, as he or she is in his or her immediate gesture. Action, so to speak, becomes detached from its agent, just as discourse does through writing in relation to speaking. This is where the question "who?" opens a real problem, one well known not only to jurists, and not just criminologists, but also to historians. Are the long-term consequences of an action still the work of their agent? This becomes an unavoidable question as soon as we distinguish in some course of events what depends on human actors and what has to be attributed either to the unintended circumstances or unintended, even perverse consequences of human action.

Another complication requires us to link intermediate actions to their immediate causes. What makes it difficult to attribute an action to some particular agent is the fact that everyone's action is not only caught up in the external course of things that happen, but it also gets incorporated into the social course of human affairs. How, when it is a case of what we can call group action are we to distinguish the part played by each of the social actors? This difficulty is a problem for the historian along with the one I mentioned earlier. And, of course, it is a problem for a judge, when it comes down to a question of how to distribute goods, rewards, or torts, that is, to distinguish among the authors distributively; here to attribute means to distribute.

These are the two directions in which one could pursue the investigation of agency, of *efficiency*. The first way leads beyond semantics. The second in a way comes back to it or even beyond it. In a word, the concept of moral and juridical imputation, to which the way that starts from above leads, implies a subject capable of designating him- or herself. The concept of power which the way that starts from below leads to points to a phenomenology of the "I can" and, even more fundamentally, to an ontology of an agent subject.

IV Ethical Implications of Action Theory

In moral philosophy, one ordinarily assumes that a teleological approach, illustrated by the Aristotelian theory of virtues, and a deontological one of duty, illustrated by Kant's ethics, are incompatible. We can call them ethics of the good and the just to designate these two traditions by means of their emblematic predicate. My goal here will be to show that a theory of action, in the broad sense, is capable of offering an appropriate conceptual framework within which we can do justice to both moments of moral life, the Aristotelian and the Kantian, the teleological and the deontological.

But instead of speaking of action, I want to talk about *praxis*, not simply out of respect for Aristotle, but in order to restore to human action its complexity and full range, something that gets easily lost from sight in what is called the "analytic philosophy of action." Only a broad sense of praxis, in my opinion, allows us to assign to the two moments of moral life two different steps on one and the same trajectory of praxis and in this way to justify their complementary relationship.

Praxis and the Teleological Moment of Moral Life

We shall proceed in the following manner. We shall consider a series of levels on the scale of praxis and ask ourselves how far it is possible to advance with a quasi-Aristotelian concept of virtue, in the sense of some excellence. By doing this, we will be able to identify the point where a quasi-Kantian model of obligation has to take over. And to suggest what will follow from this, let me suggest that it will be a consideration of violence that will impose a parallel conversion in the ethical analysis of praxis.

(a) *Practices*: I want to begin by considering four levels on the scale of praxis. I will call the first one "practices." Practices are complex actions governed by precepts of all sorts, be they technical, aesthetic, ethical, or political. The most familiar examples are professions, crafts, arts, and games. If I take the notion of a precept – or rather the applicability of a precept – as the principal criterion of a practice, in contrast to "basic actions" (to use Arthur Danto's term), we must not too quickly assign a moral sense to these precepts.[30] Not every precept is an imperative. Some are limited to offering advice, counsel, or instruction, without imposing any obligation to follow them. Nonetheless they do lie on the way to the moral imperative inasmuch as they teach us how to do well what we do. An evaluative component is implied here, one which brings an ethical analysis to the threshold of moral obligation, without for all that crossing this threshold.

We can take another step in the direction of an ethical characteristic of action, in the broad sense of the term "ethics" that

[30] Arthur Danto, "Basic Actions," *American Philosophical Quarterly* 2 (1965): 141–8.

applies to evaluative and normative codes by underscoring that practices, as distinct from mere gestures, consist in cooperative activities whose constitutive rules are socially instituted. Of course, one can play alone or garden alone, or even do laboratory research by oneself, or one can work alone in the library or in one's office, but the constitutive rules come from beyond the individual who does any of these things. The practice and learning of a skill, a game, a craft, an art, all rest on some tradition. What is more, success, excellence in carrying out such practices requires recognition by others who are skilled in the practice. This is true even if one works alone. Even outside of any form of organized competition, every practice lends itself to comparisons as a function of what we can call "standards of excellence" (a term I borrow from Alasdair MacIntyre).[31] In this sense, competition is itself an aspect of cooperation. There will be no conflict without some minimal agreement concerning the rules that define among other things the levels of success or excellence.

A new transition in action theory in the direction of moral theory – and, in truth, the real breakthrough – is assured by what I have just spoken of as standards of excellence, which govern the transmission and comparison on this plane of practices. It is true that at this stage there is not yet an established distinction between what Kant called on one side "rules governing use and advice concerning prudence," and on the other "moral maxims" in the categorial sense of this term. But the absence of this distinction is interesting in itself inasmuch as it allows the introduction, again following MacIntyre, of the notion of "immanent goods" of practice.[32] These are what a bit later will provide us with a basis for a moral theory, a place to apply these imperatives (this is also the point where I take my distance from MacIntyre). These immanent goods constitute the teleology internal to action, in the same way that the notions of interest and satisfaction give expression to it on the phenomenological level.

This notion of an *internal teleology* was already applied by Aristotle to distinguish between *poiesis*, which is a fabricating of things external to creative activity, and *praxis*, which has its

---

[31] See Alasdair MacIntyre, *After Virtue: A Study in Moral Theory* (Notre Dame, IN: University of Notre Dame Press, 1981), 177.
[32] Ibid., 178.

terminus ad quem inside such activity, as is the case for those practices that entail movement in the cases of ethical and political action. So much for my remarks concerning the first level of *praxis*.

(b) *Life plans*: We move a degree closer to the domain where the theory of action and that of morality intersect by granting a supplementary extension to the notion of practice, beyond the still limited examples of crafts, arts, and games. For example, we readily speak of a *life plan* as a way of designating those global projects, which include, for instance, professional life, family life, leisure time, etc. (we find this term "life plan" in Rawls as well as in MacIntyre). This notion allows us to return to a distinction introduced by different Aristotle specialists to account for the two levels of deliberation in the *Nichomachean Ethics*, in books III and VI. According to the means–end model in book III, the physician is already a physician, the architect already an architect. Neither one need ask if he was right to embrace the professional life designated as medicine or architecture. In contrast to this, according to the "phronetic" model in book VI, deliberation bears on the ends themselves. Its function is to specify, to make more determinate, the unclear horizon of ends and ideals that point toward what we can call the "good" life, the *true life*. Thus, we deliberate about our life ideals, whatever they may be, and the constitutive rules of this or that practice, following a back-and-forth movement.

Let us pause for a moment over this notion of a life plan, owing to the use in it of the word "life." Life is not here taken in a purely biological sense but rather in an ethico-cultural one whose use was well known to the Greeks, when they compared the respective merits of *bioi* (lives) offered to our most radical choices, those of an *anthropos* considered as a whole: the life of pleasure, the active or political life, the contemplative life. In this context, Aristotle asks whether there is an *ergon*, a function, a task for the whole human person, just as there is for the musician, the physician, the architect. Taken as a singular term, the word "life" is meant to underscore the indivisible character of an individual life.

(c) *The narrative unity of a life*: It is at this stage that we encounter a more decisive mediation between action theory and moral theory, namely, what MacIntyre calls the narrative unity of a life (rediscovering in his own way Dilthey's reflections on what he called the *Zusammenhang eines Leben*). After practices and life plans, then, comes the narrative unity of a life. In *Time and Narrative*, I was intrigued by the notion of a narrative identity that binds the notion of selfhood to that of the story or history of a life as this gets "refigured" conjointly by historiography and fiction. Today, my proposal is to situate this analysis at the point where action theory and moral theory join. This can be done, in my opinion, with the aid of two connected notions that I share with Charles Taylor, from his *Philosophical Papers*.[33] If, on the one hand, we are allowed to apply to our own lives plots and characters whose familiarity we owe to biographies and literary fictions found in our culture, this is so insofar as the practical field itself can be compared to a text offered to our reading. I refer here to my essay "The Model of the Text: Action Considered as a Text," in *From Text to Action*.[34] Anticipating his future readers, Marcel Proust writes in *Time Regained*:

> But to return to my own case, I thought more modestly of my book and it would be inaccurate to say that I thought of those who would read it as 'my' readers. For it seemed to me that they would not be 'my' readers but the readers of their own selves, my book being merely a sort of magnifying glass like those which the optician at Combray used to offer his customers – it would be my book, but with its help I would furnish them with the means of reading what lay inside themselves.[35]

"Reader of themselves," this marvelous expression indicates the inclusion even of language within the framework of action, thanks to those constitutive rules we have spoken of earlier, which authorize taking the broad units of action that we call "practices" and "life plans" as quasi-texts asking to be read. The analogy

[33] Charles Taylor, *Philosophical Papers*, vol. I: *Human Agency and Language* (New York: Cambridge University Press, 1985).
[34] Paul Ricoeur, *From Text to Action: Essays in Hermeneutics II*, trans. Kathleen Blamey and John B. Thompson (Evanston: Northwestern University Press, 1991), 144–67.
[35] Marcel Proust, *In Search of Lost Time*, vol. VI: *Time Regained*, trans. Andreas Mayor and Terence Kilmartin, rev. D. J. Enright (New York: Modern Library, 1993), 508.

applies here at the level of composition, of configuration that applies both to a text and such quasi-texts. As a quasi-text, action derives its readability from the rules that connect it together, thanks to which we can say that in raising our hand, we vote; that in leaving a room we break off negotiations; in running down the street we take part in a riot; and so on.

The second notion implied here, beyond that of a quasi-text, is that of interpretation taken in the sense of a self-interpretation. We have several reasons for introducing this term at this moment in our analysis. First of all, the quasi-text of an action, like every other text, makes room for a kind of hermeneutic circle, inasmuch as one interprets it as a whole as a function of its parts and vice versa. Yet this is still a trivial point. In the second place, we need to take into account that the action has a signification only for someone who interprets himself in interpreting the text of the action. The concept of agent correlative with that of action is enriched in this manner. The agent is the author of his action inasmuch as he interprets himself as a function of the capacities, skills, games in which he engages in conformity with the competence and degrees of excellence determined by their constitutive rules. In this sense, Charles Taylor speaks of human beings as self-interpreting animals. A third function of the concept on interpretation on the level of practices is to underscore the role of challenges and rivalry in the exercising of judgments regarding excellence.

As soon as we have to do with significations or, better, a significance (that is, a signification for someone), there is a place for controversy. The epistemological consequence is clear: to interpret ourselves, to interpret a practice overall does not leave room for the kind of procedures of verification that we can expect from a science based on observation. The adequacy of an interpretation rests on an exercise of judgment that, in the best cases, can only be taken as plausible.

(d) *A true life*: The fourth and final degree of *praxis* is that of a "good life." I would like to conclude this progression in the direction of strictly moral considerations by introducing a final practical concept, that of a "good life," which translates the Greek *euzoia, eu zèn*. Aristotle makes a clear distinction between the Platonic idea of the Good and "good for human beings," in order to indicate the unclear horizon for ideals and dreams of accomplishing them, as a function of which a life can be can as more or less complete. It is the good life, the *true life*, to use a term dear to Proust. With this concept, the evaluative point of view wins out over the strictly descriptive one in the domain of action. The true life constitutes the horizon offered to a progressive series constituted by the notions of constitutive rules, standards of excellence, life plans, and the narrative unity of a life. Rather than horizon, we could have spoken of a limit-idea to characterize the relation between the notion of a true life and the teleologically oriented series of intermediary notions capable of connecting action theory and moral theory.

Praxis and the Deonotological Moment of a Moral Life

I shall begin with the word brought up without any preparation at the end of the preceding section. Because there is violence, I said, there is morality (and I will add by way of anticipation, politics). I shall add to this word two equally abrupt affirmations. Because there is violence, morality cannot confine itself to preferences, wishes, *evaluations* stated in the *optative* mode. It has to be prescriptive, that is, to speak in an imperative mode about obligations and prohibitions. Violence, in effect, exceeds what should not be wished for, because it is evil – perhaps Evil – it ought not to be, and its limitation, if it cannot be completely suppressed, is of the order of a *devoir-être, ought, sollen*. Let us add: because there is violence, the other than oneself is projected to the center of ethics, be he the victim, the hangman, the witness, the judge. This reference to other people does not have the same necessity, the same urgency in a purely *evaluative* approach to *praxis* internally animated by the goal of "living well." The care of the self, guided by those kinds of excellences in the accomplishment of an action that are the virtues, can turn into a haughty egoism shielded from the disasters that must lead to the care of others. Stoic *ataraxia* – to which I do not mean to reduce the whole history of eudemonism – today requires its adherents to close their ears so as not to hear the weeping of children or the cries of the tortured. Because there is violence, there is morality with its prescriptions and prohibitions, its being haunted by others.

But what does "there is" mean when it is a question of morals? To say there is morality is to say that the task of the philosopher is not to create all its pieces, drawing them out of nothingness. We are born and live in a society where laws are in force, where norms have been stated, where imperatives have already been announced, which we respond to through obedience or disobedience. This means, that even before doing any philosophy, we have already understood what "you must... you must not" (lie, kill) means. The philosopher's task is rather to reflect on some of the exemplary norms, recognized by most people, and starting from there to move back toward the source of obligation. Moral philosophy has never worked in any other way. Aristotle, in his two books on ethics, starts from a broad consensus, from *endoxa*, that is, those ideas accepted by most people concerning the major virtues and their relation to the quest for happiness. The philosopher limits himself to clarifying, correcting, and if necessary criticizing what he has neither an ambition nor the means to draw simply from himself. Kant, even more openly, declares at the beginning of the first section of his *Groundwork for a Metaphysic of Morals*: "It is impossible to think of anything at all that could be considered good without limitation (*für gut... gehalten*)... except a *good will*."[36] His *Metaphysics of Morals*, in this regard, has no other ambition but to put this idea to the test (*auf die Prüfung stellen*), and to reflect on the conditions of a good will.[37]

In what terms should we then formulate the principle of morality? Following Alan Donagan, in his *The Theory of Morality*,[38] I will adopt as a guideline, not exactly the second formulation of the Kantian imperative, but a more primitive principle, in both a historical and a rational sense, namely, the Golden Rule as we find it formulated by Hillel, Saint Paul's Jewish teacher: "Do not do to your neighbor what you would not like him to do to you.

[36] Immanuel Kant, *Groundwork for the Metaphysics of Morals*, in *Practical Philosophy*, The Cambridge Edition of the Works of Immanuel Kant, trans. and ed. Mary J. Gregor (Cambridge: Cambridge University Press, 1996), 49.
[37] Immanuel Kant, *The Metaphysics of Morals*, trans. and ed. Mary J. Gregor (Cambridge: Cambridge University Press, 1996).
[38] Alan Donagan, *The Theory of Morality* (Chicago: University of Chicago Press, 1977).

This is the whole law; everything else is commentary" (Babylonian Talmud 31a). We read something similar in the Gospel of Matthew: "In everything do to others as you would have them do to you" (7:12), or more briefly in Luke 10:25–8: "you shall love your neighbor as yourself," drawing on Leviticus 19:18.

The golden rule immediately confers an intersubjective dimension on the principle of morality, and not just any one at all. I want to emphasize this point.

That an intersubjective dimension is inherent in the golden rule corrects a certain tendency toward solipsism in action theory. The theory of basic actions, which refers, I said at the end of my third section, to the lived experience that "I can," does not take into account our relation to other agents. But this is not what is most important. For, after all, nothing prevents action theory from developing itself into a theory of interaction, as we see in Max Weber and Alfred Schutz. This extension is even implicit in the notion of "practice" in that, as we emphasized earlier, it includes the possibility of cooperation and competition. Yet, the principle of morality goes much further than this. To the extent that it accents, not just the conflictual side of interaction, but the essential asymmetry between what we call a fact, doing something, and what is done to another; in other words, what the other undergoes: "what you would not like him to do to you." In this sense, the principle of morality does not set side-by-side, or face-to-face, two agents, but an agent and a patient of some action. A patient – someone to whom something is done. To dramatize this asymmetry, this initial inequality, we could say that the other is potentially the victim of my action, just as he is possibly my adversary. Here is a good reason to admire Hillel's formulation: "what you would not like him to do to you." This aspect of otherness of the other should not be underestimated to the benefit of some hypostasis of the other as a figure of the teacher of justice. Even the prophet's voice that says to me "thou shall not kill" is virtually the voice of the suffering servant who says "do not kill me." My judge is first of all my victim. It is in this sense that I risk saying that morality is our response to violence.

This proposition can be taken in a sense that weakens its import. We might read it as: morality is our response to the violence of others. This could legitimate a political, even a juridical philosophy, but not a moral philosophy, which in the first place puts me in the potential position of being the violent one, with the other in the position of being the victim. This way of eluding the sharp edge of the principle of morality is familiar from the tradition of natural law, where the other figures above all as someone who can interfere with my rights, that is, in the last analysis, with my power to act. In this way, the other is potentially an aggressor against me rather than my victim. For example, for Hobbes, as Leo Strauss forcefully shows, the fear of a violent death constitutes the ultimate passion that motivates handing over my inherent rights to some absolute monarch.[39] In other classical theories of natural law, the first appearance of the other is less dramatic. It comes down to the threat of interference in my private sphere of interests, in ways that hinder my ability to act rather than threaten my death. Nonetheless, this suffices to depict the other as an equal adversary, rather than an unequal victim. In this regard, the golden rule is more perspicuous. It sees in the first agent, the one to whom it is addressed, someone who claims a power *over* someone else and who, as a result, treats this other person as someone submitted to his or her power. It is in this sense that morality and violence are contemporary with each other, and, if I may put it this way, coextensive.

But before moving on, we need to consider a well-known objection that applies to the golden rule, as well as to its Kantian reformulation. Such a formal rule, it has often been said, must be empty, that is, it lacks application to singular cases stemming from this rule. The answer I will give to this objection directly governs the attempt I made in my third section to integrate the evaluative dimension, considered in the preceding section, into the normative dimension properly speaking of the preceding section. My answer is twofold. First, the formal character of the golden rule is its strength, not its weakness. It leaves room for moral invention that discovers what in each situation "counts as" (objectively) allowed or (subjectively) blamable. Here is where Aristotelian *phronesis* regains its place, as deliberation bearing both on the interpretation of the situation and on the kind of rule that fits, *hic et nunc*. Having said this, there would exist an unbearable hiatus between

---

[39] Leo Strauss, *The Political Philosophy of Hobbes: Its Basis and Its Genesis*, trans. Elsa M. Sinclair (Chicago: University of Chicago Press, 1952).

the formal rule and moral judgment in any specific situation, if some transition in the direction of singular cases were not prescribed by the rule itself. Here we touch on one of the most controversial points in the exegesis of Kant's texts. It has to do with the articulation of the rule in terms of some well-known "examples" (returning a loaned object, speaking the truth to robbers, etc.). I agree with Donagan that the principle of morality, however formal it may be, is not empty inasmuch as the formal rule and a judgment applied to a situation interweave what Donagan calls additional premises, or more precisely "specifying" ones, whose function is to "identify a kind of action as falling or not falling under the fundamental generic concept of action in which every human being is respected as being a rational creature."[40] The most appropriate model is provided by jurisprudence, as Emilio Betti has made clear in his own book on hermeneutics.[41] In a similar sense, Donagan points to the testimony of the jurist and philosopher Edward H. Levi.[42] According to Levi, the chain of judicial reasoning takes the form of a "circular motion" that passes through three stages. First a legal concept is created on the basis of numerous cases. Then this more or less fixed concept is applied to new cases, until – the third stage – a breaking point is reached under the pressure of new cases that requires the creation of a new concept. The whole difficulty lies in establishing and the logical functioning of these "specifying" premises.[43]

That there always are such specifying premises in moral judgments is beyond doubt. The principle of morality is always applied through interpretations that limit its import. For example, the rule "thou shall not kill" has always and everywhere given rise to exceptions, among which the least debatable are those having to do with a legitimate defense, particularly when threatened with death. The counterpart to this limitation is specifying murder as the act of killing someone outside these allowed exceptions. But it is precisely the specificity of the general rule with its exceptions

---

[40] Donagan, *The Theory of Morality*, 68.
[41] Emilio Betti, *Die Hermeneutik as allgemeine Methodik der Geisteswissenschaften* (Tübigen: J. C. B. Mohr, 1962).
[42] Edward H. Levi, *An Introduction to Legal Reasoning* (Chicago: University of Chicago Press, 1949).
[43] Donagan, *The Theory of Morality*, 68.

that gets underway the process of revision through which new cases call for new specifying premises. Let me offer an example. Through the centuries, slaves did not count as members of the group defined as those who are truly human, that is, the group of free people to whom the formal rule of respect due to every rational creature applied. The specifying premise that served as an obstacle was one that extended the right to own property to people who were purchased in certain conditions, and that at the same time defined rational creatures as those who were free. It was this premise that was abandoned owing to different pressures, some of which were specifically moral. Therefore it was necessary, through public deliberation, to construct a new premise by virtue of which it fell to slaves the right to exercise all the liberties recognized up until that point as belonging to free people. It was this category of only some being free people, functioning as a specifying premise, that lost its credibility as soon as its limiting role was seen to contradict the initial force that led to the expansion of an underlying moral premise.

In this way, rational deliberation can interweave itself between the formal rule of the respect due to other people and to oneself, and singular moral decisions. It is what has governed, and continues to govern, moral casuistry and jurisprudence, by the principle of adherence to precedents. We can grasp its functioning in new cases where a consensus is in the process of being elaborated; as yesterday with regard to abortion, today and tomorrow with regard to genetic manipulations, and always with regard to torture, the rights of civilians and prisoners in times of war, and in every case of an attack on our liberty.

The Taking Up of Evaluative Judgment into Normative Judgment

My thesis, that the principal mediation between the principle of morality and singular moral decisions is assured by the taking up of the evaluations immanent in *praxis* in the course of deliberation, finds its basis in the golden rule, for which I have not as yet pointed out an important feature that distinguishes it from the apparently equivalent Kantian formulation. The golden rule says: "Do not do to others what you would not like them to do to you." To this point, we have emphasized the intersubjective side of this principle. But we have neglected the affective side, expressed by the terms "not like" and "like." Referring to feelings as strong as liking or hating takes nothing away from the formal aspect of the golden rule. What actions we would not like are not specified. But the reference to goods and evils, in the sense of experienced satisfactions and sufferings, means that the rule can remain formal without becoming empty. What we immediately speak of are goods and evils in the plural. In order to maintain the relation between love and hate within the formal limits of the moral rule, therefore, our inquiry has to bear precisely on what Alan Donagan calls "fundamental human goods."[44] These goods are fundamental in the sense that they are not the object of arbitrary wishes, following the Kantian description of desire as pathological. They are contingent goods, to be sure, but ones without which the exercise of free choice and the development of a life governed by rational intentions would be impossible. In this regard the golden rule is more considerate – as I suggested earlier – than its Kantian counterpart. It leaves open the option between an ethic of the good and goods and one of obligation. I claim that it even authorizes the integration of the latter into the former. Indeed, it is not by chance that the notion of fundamental human goods suggested by the golden rule links up with that of the goods immanent to some practice, to which I devoted a major part of the preceding section. There we assigned this notion to the plane of appreciative or evaluative judgments. One result is that, thanks to their coincidence with the notion of fundamental human goods, practices can assume a normative function. In this way, the golden rule becomes the standard by which we measure the conformity between those goods immanent to some practice and fundamental human goods, concerning which there is a broad consensus on the plane of common moral beliefs. We may formulate this sought-for convergence in the following terms: "Act in such a way that the optative goods your practice aims at should conform to the normative goods implied by the principle of morality." This coincidence between the evaluative judgments immanent to *praxis* and the normative judgments implied by the golden rule having to do with human goods assures the intersection between action and moral theory.

[44] Ibid., 61.

I am well aware of the resistance this attempt to bring about conciliation between an ethics of virtue in an Aristotelian style and an ethics of duty in a Kantian style may encounter. Earlier I spoke of the reasons why it is necessary to pass from an optative moral philosophy to one based on duty. They are summed up by the necessity to oppose morality to violence, a problem not found in Aristotle, who, to repeat, recognizes only that violence an agent suffers, but not that violence that an agent exercises against someone else. What needs to be acknowledged, in the opposite direction, is what seems to be an obstacle to integrating the optative into the normative. What seems to prevent this sought-for integration is first the puritanical evaluation of desire in Kant. But we set this aside by putting violence in the place of desire. Next there is his refusal of any diversity among and of a hierarchy of feelings which leads him to reduce love to "pathological" desire. In this way, the ethics of the categorical imperative finds itself arbitrarily cut off from any legitimate search for satisfaction, for a sense of accomplishment, in a word for seeking a "good life" in the Greek sense of this term. The unique norm is thereby stripped of the specific mediation that those patrons of excellence, the virtues could offer it – I mean those habitual responses, those dispositions applied in an appropriate manner to human situations that are themselves generic and fundamental. For example, temperance in the use of pleasures and pains (Pascal: "The good use of misfortunes"),[45] liberality in the exercise of kindness, friendship in the reciprocal exchange of esteem, justice with regard to the unequal distribution of advantages and disadvantages in social life, and so on. Kant, to be sure, is right to call the love of neighbor practical in the sense that this love is nothing if it does not consist in treating the other according to the duty of respect. But love for all that is still a feeling, as Kant grants when he deals with respect (*Achtung*). But respect is not addressed only to others, as the seat of the moral law, but also to an other who has interests, who aims at a "good life" which depends on the contingent acquisition and conservation of goods that can slip from his grasp. In this sense, to respect others is to want their good, to wish for their satisfaction, and good luck! In this way, I find myself in agreement with Donagan when he rewrites the

[45] Blaise Pascal, "Prière pour demander à Dieu le bon usage des maladies," in *Œuvres complètes*, ed. L. Lafuma (Paris: Seuil, 1963), 362–5.

second formulation of the Kantian imperative as "act so that the fundamental human goods, whether in your own person or in that of another, are promoted as may be possible, and under no circumstances violated."[46] The notion of fundamental human goods gets put in the same place as the concept of "humanity" in the Kantian reformulation of the golden rule; in the same place, but with a new function that the idea of humanity cannot satisfy, that of procuring a plurality of guidelines for the application of the principles of morality to particular cases. In my opinion, the epistemological function of the notion of fundamental human goods is to provide the mediation starting from which *phronesis* ["practical wisdom"] and the *phronimos* ["the person who has *phronesis*"] deliberate in singular situations and in the presence of new cases. The respective places for coherence and invention are preserved in this way.

I do not want to conclude this section without having added two corollaries that accentuate the distance of the present attempt from Kant. By insisting on the contingent character of fundamental human goods, I have emphasized a double feature of the moral life for which Aristotle has done better justice than did Kant: on the one hand, the *fragility* of human *praxis* in regard to what the Ancients called fortune and the Moderns call chance; on the other, the vulnerability with regard to recurrent *violence* that makes human agents in turn victim or executioner (without adding with the poet: "the knife and the scar").[47] This double contingency of the goods on which "good" praxis hangs means the rule of justice is indiscernible from the moral rule.[48]

---

[46] Donagan, *The Theory of Morality*, 61.

[47] A reference to Baudelaire's poem "L'Héautontimorouménos," in *Les Fleurs du mal*, lxxxiii, 85; *The Flowers of Evil*, 105.

[48] Kant's inability to take this contingency into account is a result of his method in the *Critique of Practical Reason*, which transposes – for no good reason, in my opinion – the distinction between *a priori* and *a posteriori* from the theoretical to the practical sphere. By doing this, duty is split off from desire and, still more grave, the moral aspect of the most basic conditions is cut off from the exercising of *praxis*. This is why I find more to think about in *The Groundwork of the Metaphysics of Morals* than in the *Critique of Practical Reason*, inasmuch as the former work is less governed and, if I can put it so, less crushed by the concern to draw a line separating a priori and a posteriori across practice. – Ricoeur's note.

Second corollary: By conferring on the notion of "fundamental human goods" a mediating role between the moral rule and singular judgments, we leave open the possibility that the derivation of moral principles will run into real conflicts, as a result of the qualitative plurality of those very fundamental human goods themselves that guide this derivation. In this sense, the notion of a conflict of duties does not seem to me something that can be eliminated from the practical sphere. There is here an important limit to the deductive claim, with its ambition of coherence, if not of forming a system, in rational moral philosophy, and a serious argument in favor of moral invention, if not of improvisation, as in the case made at length by Gadamer.

2

Metaphor and the Central Problem of Hermeneutics

We shall assume here that the central problem of hermeneutics is that of interpretation.[1] Not interpretation in some undetermined sense of the word, but interpretation in two determinate ways: the first one has to do with its field of application, the second its epistemological specificity. As regards the first point, I shall say that there is a problem of interpretation because there are texts, written texts, the autonomy of which create specific difficulties. By "autonomy" I understand the independence of the text with respect to its author's intention, its original setting, and its original reader. These problems are resolved in oral discourse through the kind of exchange or interaction we call dialogue or

[1] This essay first appeared in the *Revue Philosophique du Louvain* 70 (1972): 93–115. An unattributed English translation of this essay, here slightly revised to reflect its publication in the French edition of this volume, appeared in the *Graduate Faculty Philosophy Journal* 3 (1973–1974): 42–58; reprinted in *New Literary History* 6 (1974–1975): 95–110; *The Philosophy of Paul Ricoeur: An Anthology of His Work*, ed. Charles E. Reagan and David Stewart (Boston: Beacon Press/Toronto: Fitzhenry and Whiteside Limited, 1978), 134–48; Paul Ricoeur, *Hermeneutics and the Human Sciences: Essays on Language, Action, and Interpretation*, ed. John B. Thompson (Cambridge: Cambridge University Press, 1981), 165–81; *Philosophy Looks at the Arts: Contemporary Readings in Aesthetics*, ed. Joseph Margolis (Philadelphia: Temple University Press, 1987), 577–92.

conversation. With written texts, discourse must speak for itself. Let us say, therefore, that there are problems of interpretation because the writing–reading relation is not a particular case of the speaking–hearing relation that we experience in the dialogical situation. This is the most general feature of interpretation as regards its field of application.

Second, the concept of interpretation, at the epistemological level, appears to be opposed to the concept of explanation. Taken together, these two concepts form a contrasting pair that has given rise to a great many disputes since the time of Schleiermacher and Dilthey. According to this tradition, interpretation has some specific subjective connotations, such as the implication of the reader in the processes of understanding and the reciprocity between interpretation of the text and self-interpretation. This reciprocity is known by the name of the "hermeneutical circle"; it implies a sharp opposition to the sort of objectivity and non-implication that is supposed to characterize the scientific explanation of things. Below I shall say to what extent we may be able to amend, indeed reconstruct on a new basis, the opposition between interpretation and explanation. Whatever the outcome of that subsequent discussion may be, this schematic description of the concept of interpretation suffices for a provisional circumscription of the central problem of hermeneutics: the status of written texts *versus* spoken language, the status of interpretation *versus* explanation.

Now for metaphor!

The aim of this essay is to connect the problems raised in hermeneutics by the interpretation of texts and the problems raised in rhetoric, semantics, stylistics – or whatever the discipline concerned may be – by way of metaphor.

Text and Metaphor as Discourse

Our first task will be to find a common ground for the theory of the text and the theory of metaphor. This common ground has already received a name – discourse; it has yet to be given a status.

To begin, one thing is striking: the two sorts of entities we are considering are of different lengths. In this respect, we can compare them to the basic unit of discourse, the sentence. A text can undoubtedly be reduced to a single sentence, as in proverbs or aphorisms; but texts have a maximum length that can extend from a paragraph to a chapter, a book, a collection of "selected works," or even the corpus of the "complete works" of an author. Let us use the term "work" to describe the closed sequence of discourse that can be considered as a text. Whereas texts can be identified on the basis of their maximal length, metaphors can be identified on the basis of their minimal length, that of a word. If the rest of this discussion is meant to show that there is no metaphor – in the sense of a word taken metaphorically – in the absence of certain contexts, and consequently if we are constrained by what follows to replace the notion of metaphor by that of metaphorical statement which implies at least the length of the sentence, nevertheless the "metaphorical twist" (to speak like Monroe Beardsley) is something that happens to the word.[2] The change of meaning, which requires the full contribution of the context, affects the word. We can then describe the word as having a "metaphorical use" or a "non-literal meaning"; it is in this sense that the word is always the bearer of the "emergent meaning" that specific contexts confer upon it. In this sense, Aristotle's definition of metaphor – as the odd transposition of an unusual word name (or word) – is not invalidated by a theory that emphasizes the contextual action which creates the shift of the word's meaning.[3] The word remains the "focus," even if the focus requires the "frame" of the sentence, to use the vocabulary of Max Black. This first, strictly formal remark concerning the difference in length between the text and the metaphor, or better, between the *work* and the *word*, is going to help us elaborate our initial problem in a more precise way: to what extent can we treat the metaphor as a *work in miniature*? The answer to this question will then help us to pose a second question: to what extent can the hermeneutical problems raised by the interpretation of texts be considered as a large-scale extension of the problems condensed in the explanation of a local metaphor in a given text?

Is a metaphor a work in miniature? Can a work, let us say a poem, be considered as a sustained or extended metaphor? The

[2] Monroe Beardsley, "The Metaphorical Twist," *Philosophy and Phenomenological Research* 22 (1962): 293–307.
[3] Aristotle, *Poetics*, 1457b.

answer to this first question requires a prior elaboration of the general properties of discourse, if it is true that text and metaphor, work and word, fall within the same category of discourse. I shall not elaborate in detail the concept of discourse, but limit my analysis to those features necessary for the comparison between text and metaphor. It is remarkable that all these features present themselves in the form of paradoxes, that is, apparent contradictions.

To begin with, all discourse is produced as an event; as such, it is the counterpart of language understood as a code or system; as an event it has a fleeting existence: it appears and disappears. But at the same time – and herein lies the paradox – it can be identified and re-identified as the same. This "sameness" is what we call, in a broad sense, its meaning. Discourse, we shall say, is realized as event but understood as meaning. We shall soon see in what sense the metaphor condenses this double character of event and meaning.

The second pair of contrasting features stems from the fact that meaning is supported by a specific structure, that of the proposition, which envelops an internal opposition between a pole of singular identification (this man, this table, Mr Smith, Paris) and a pole of general predication (humanity as a class, brightness as a property, equality as a relation, running as an action). Metaphor, we shall also see, rests upon this "attribution" of characteristics to the "principal subject" of a sentence.

The third pair of opposing features is the polarity, which discourse, primarily in its sentential form, implies between sense and reference, that is, the possibility of distinguishing between *what* is said by the sentence taken as a whole and by the words as parts of the sentence – and *that about which* something is said. To speak is to say something about something. This polarity will play a decisive role in the second and third parts of this essay, where I shall try to connect the problem of explanation to the dimension of "sense," that is, the immanent pattern of discourse, and the problem of interpretation to the dimension of "reference," understood as the power of discourse to apply to an extra-linguistic reality about which it says what it says.

Fourth, discourse, as an act, can be considered from the point of view of the "contents" of the propositional act (it predicates a certain characteristic of a certain subject), or from the point of view of what Austin called the "force" of the complete act of discourse (the *speech-act* in his terminology). What is said of the subject is one thing. What I "do" *in* speaking is another: I can make a mere description, or give an order, or formulate a wish, or give a warning, etc.[4] Whence the polarity between the locutionary act (the act *of* saying) and the illocutionary act (what I do *in* saying). This polarity may seem less useful than the preceding ones, at least at the structural level of the metaphorical statement; nevertheless, it will play a decisive role when we have to place the metaphor back in its concrete setting, for example, a poem, an essay, or a work of fiction.

Before developing the dichotomy of sense and reference as the basis of the opposition between explanation and interpretation, let us introduce a final polarity that will play a decisive role in hermeneutical theory. Discourse has not just one sort of reference but two: it refers to an extra-linguistic reality, let us say the world or a world; and it refers equally to its own speaker, by means of specific procedures that function only in the sentence, therefore only in discourse: for example, the personal pronouns, verb tenses, demonstratives, etc.

In this way, language has both a reference to reality and a self-reference. It is the same entity – the sentence – that supports this double intentional and reflexive reference, turned toward the thing and toward the self. In truth, we should speak of a triple reference, for discourse refers as much to the one to whom it is addressed as to its own speaker. The structure of the personal pronouns, as Emile Benveniste taught, conveys this triple reference: "it" designates the reference to the thing, "you" the reference to the one to whom the discourse is addressed, and "I" the reference to the one who speaks.[5] As we shall see below, this connection between two and even three directions of reference will provide us with the key to the hermeneutical circle and the basis for our reinterpretation of this circle.

I will list these basic polarities of discourse in the following condensed fashion: event and meaning, singular identification and

[4] See John L. Austin, *How to Do Things with Words* (Oxford: Clarendon Press, 1962).
[5] See Emile Benveniste, "The Nature of Pronouns," in *Problems in General Linguistics*, trans. Mary Elizabeth Meek (Coral Gables, FL: University of Miami Press, 1971), 217–22.

general predication, propositional act and illocutionary act, sense and reference, reference to reality and reference to interlocutors.

In what sense can we now say that the text and metaphor both rest upon the sort of entity we have just called discourse?

It is easy to show that all texts are discourses, since they stem from the smallest unit of discourse, the sentence. A text is at least a series of sentences. We shall see in what follows that it must be something more if it is to be a work. But it is at minimum a set of sentences, consequently a discourse. The connection between metaphor and discourse requires a special justification, precisely because the definition of metaphor as a transposition affecting names or words seems to place it in a category of entities smaller than the sentence. But the semantics of the word demonstrates very clearly that words acquire an actual meaning only in a sentence and that lexical entities – the words in the dictionary – have merely potential meanings, depending on their potential uses in typical contexts. In this respect, the theory of polysemy is a good preparation for the theory of metaphor. At the lexical level, words, if they can already be called that, have more than one meaning; it is only by a specific contextual action of sifting that they realize, in a given sentence, a part of their potential semantics and acquire what we call a determinate meaning. The contextual action that enables univocal discourse to be produced with polysemic words is the model for that other contextual action whereby we draw genuinely novel metaphorical effects from words whose meaning is already codified in the lexicon. In this way, we are prepared to allow that even if the meaningful effect we call metaphor is inscribed in the word, the origin of this effect lies in a contextual action that places the semantic fields of several words in interaction.

As regards the metaphor itself, semantics shows with the same force that the metaphorical meaning of a word cannot be found in the dictionary. In this sense, we can continue to oppose the metaphorical to the literal meaning, on the condition of calling the literal meaning *any* of the meanings we can find among the partially codified meanings of the lexicon. By literal meaning, therefore, we do not mean a supposedly original, fundamental, primitive, or proper meaning of a word among the meanings assigned to a word on the lexical level; the literal meaning is the totality of the semantic field, the set of possible contextual uses that constitutes the polysemy of a word. So if the metaphorical meaning is something more and other than the actualization of one of the possible meanings of a polysemic word (and all the words in natural languages are polysemic), this metaphorical use has to be be solely contextual: in saying this, I mean a meaning that emerges as the unique and fleeting result of a certain contextual action. We are led in this way to oppose contextual changes of meaning to the lexical changes that apply to the diachronic aspect of language as code, system, of *langue*. Metaphor is one such contextual change of meaning.

In saying this, I am partially in agreement with the modern theory of metaphor, as elaborated in English by I. A. Richards, Max Black, Monroe Beardsley, Douglas Berggren, etc.[6] More precisely, I agree with these authors on the fundamental point: a word receives a metaphorical meaning in specific contexts, within which it is opposed to other words taken literally; this shift in meaning results principally from a clash of literal meanings, which excludes the literal use of the word in question and provides clues for finding a new meaning capable of fitting into the context of the sentence and rendering it meaningful in the given context. Hence, I retain the following points from this recent history of the problem of metaphor: the replacement of the rhetorical theory of substitution by a properly semantic theory of the interaction of semantic fields; the decisive role of semantic clash leading to logical absurdity; the emergence of a particle of meaning that renders the sentence as a whole meaningful.

Let us now say how this properly semantic theory – or interaction theory – satisfies the principal characteristics we have recognized in discourse.

First, let us return to the contrast between event and meaning. In the metaphorical statement (we shall no longer speak of metaphor as a word but as a sentence), the contextual action creates

---

[6] I. A. Richards, *The Philosophy of Rhetoric* (New York: Oxford University Press, 1936); Max Black, *Models and Metaphors* (Ithaca: Cornell University Press, 1962); Monroe Beardsley, *Aesthetics: Problems in the Philosophy of Criticism* (New York: Harcourt, Brace and World, 1958), [reprinted (Indianapolis: Hackett, 1988)]; "The Metaphorical Twist"; Douglas Berggren, "The Use and Abuse of Metaphor, I and II," *Review of Metaphysics* 16 (1962): 237–58, 450–72. – Ricoeur's note, with the one addition.

a new meaning that is indeed an event, since it exists only in this particular context. But at the same time, it can be identified as the same, since it can be repeated. Hence, the innovation of an "emergent meaning" (Beardsley) may be regarded as a linguistic creation; but if it is adopted by an influential part of the language community, it may in turn become an everyday meaning and get added to the polysemy of lexical entities, contributing in this way to the history of language as *langue*, code, or system. Yet, at this final stage, when the meaningful effect we call metaphor has joined the change of meaning that augments polysemy, the metaphor is no longer living but dead. Only genuine, that is, live metaphors are at the same time "event" *and* "meaning."

The contextual action requires in the same way our second polarity, that between singular identification and general predication: A metaphor is said of a "principal subject"; as "modifier" of this subject, it works as a kind of "attribution." All the theories I have just referred to rest upon this predicative structure, whether they oppose "vehicle" to "tenor" (Richards), "frame" to "focus" (Max Black), or "modifier" to "principal subject" (Beardsley).

To show that metaphor requires the polarity between sense and reference will require a whole section of this essay; the same must be said of the polarity between reference to reality and reference to self. Below it will become clear why, at this stage, I am not in a position to say more about these polarities of sense and reference and reference to reality and reference to self. The mediation of the theory of the text will be required in order to discern those oppositions that do not appear so clearly within the narrow limits of a simple metaphorical statement.

Having delimited the field of comparison in this way, however, we are ready for the second step in which I will propose to answer our second question: to what extent can the explanation and interpretation of texts, on the one hand, and the explanation and interpretation of metaphors, on the other, be taken as similar processes, which are merely applied to two different strategic levels of discourse, the level of the work and that of the word?

From Metaphor to Text: Explanation

I propose to explore a working hypothesis which, to begin with, I shall simply state. From one point of view, the understanding of metaphor can serve as a guide to the understanding of longer texts, such as a literary work. This point of view is that of explanation; it concerns only that aspect of meaning which we have called the "sense," that is, the immanent pattern of discourse. From another point of view, the understanding of a work taken as a whole gives the key to metaphor. This other point of view is that of interpretation proper; it develops the aspect of meaning which we have called "reference," that is, the intentional orientation towards a world and the reflexive orientation towards a self. So if we apply explanation to "sense," as the immanent pattern of the work, we can reserve interpretation for the sort of inquiry concerned with the *power of a work* to project a world of its own and to set in motion the hermeneutical circle, which encompasses in its spiral both the apprehension of projected worlds and the advance of self-understanding in the presence of these new worlds. Our working hypothesis thus invites us to proceed from the metaphor to text at the level of "sense" and the explanation of "sense," then from the text to metaphor at the level of the reference of a work to a world and to a self, that is, at the level of interpretation proper.

What aspects of the explanation of metaphor can serve as a paradigm for the explanation of a text? These aspects are features of the explanatory process which could not appear so long as trivial examples of metaphor were considered, such as man is a wolf, a fox, a lion (if we read the best authors on metaphor, we observe interesting variations within the bestiary which provides them with examples!). With these examples, we elude the major difficulty; that of *identifying a meaning* which is *new*. The only way of achieving this identification is to construct a meaning which alone enables us to make sense of the sentence as a whole. For what do trivial metaphors rest upon? Max Black and Monroe Beardsley note that the meaning of a word does not depend merely on the semantic and syntactic rules that govern its literal use, but also on other rules (which are nevertheless rules) to which the members of a language community are "committed" and which determine what Black calls the "system of associated commonplaces" and Beardsley the "potential range of connotations." In the statement, "man is a wolf" (the example favored by Black!), the principal subject is qualified by one of the features of animal life that belongs to "the lupine system of associated commonplaces." The system of implications operates like a filter or screen;

it does not merely select, but also accentuates new aspects of the principal subject.

What are we to think of this explanation in relation to our description of metaphor as a new meaning appearing in a new context? As I said above, I entirely agree with the "interaction view" implied by this explanation; metaphor is more than a simple substitution whereby one word would replace another literal word, which an exhaustive paraphrase could restore to the same place. The algebraic sum of these two operations – substitution by the speaker and restoration by the author or reader – is equal to zero. No new meaning emerges and we learn nothing. As Black says, " 'interaction-metaphors' are not expendable.... This use of a 'subsidiary subject' to foster insight into a 'principal subject is a distinctive intellectual operation.' Hence interaction metaphors cannot be translated into direct language without 'a loss in cognitive content.' "[7]

Although this account describes very well the meaningful effect of metaphor, we must ask whether, by simply adding the "system of associated commonplaces" and cultural rules to the semantic polysemy of the word and semantic rules, this account does justice to the power of metaphor "to inform and enlighten." Is not the "system of associated commonplaces" something dead or at least something already established? Of course, this system must intervene in some way or another, in order that contextual action may be regulated and that the construction of new meaning may obey some prescription. Black's theory reserves the possibility that "metaphors can be supported by specially constructed systems of implications, as well as by accepted commonplaces."[8] The problem is precisely that of these "specially constructed systems of implications." We must therefore pursue our investigation into the process of interaction itself, if we are to explain the case of new metaphors in new contexts.

Beardsley's theory of metaphor leads us a stage further in this direction. If, following him, we emphasize the role of logical absurdity or the clash between literal meanings within the same context, then we are ready to recognize the genuinely creative character of metaphorical meaning: "In poetry, the principle tactic

[7] Black, *Models and Metaphors*, 46. – Ricoeur's note.
[8] Ibid., 43. – Ricoeur's note.

for obtaining this result is logical absurdity."[9] Logical absurdity creates a situation in which we have the choice of either preserving the literal meaning of the subject and the modifier and hence concluding that the entire sentence is absurd, or attributing a new meaning to the modifier so that the sentence as a whole makes sense. We are faced not only with "self-contradictory" attribution, but with a "meaningful self-contradictory" attribution. If I say "man is a fox" (the fox has chased away the wolf!), I must slide from a literal to a metaphorical attribution if I want to save the sentence. But from where do we draw this new meaning?

As long as we ask this type of question – "from where do we draw...?" – we return to the same type of ineffectual answer. The "potential range of connotations" says nothing more than the "system of associated commonplaces." Of course, we expand the notion of meaning by including "secondary meanings," as connotations, within the perimeter of full meaning; but we continue to bind the creative process of metaphor to a non-creative aspect of language.

Is it sufficient to supplement this "potential range of connotations," as Beardsley does in the "revised verbal-opposition theory,"[10] with the properties that do not yet belong to the range of connotations of my language? At first sight, this supplementation improves the theory; as Beardsley forcefully says, "metaphor transforms a *property* (actual or attributed) into a *sense*."[11]

This change is important, since it must now be said that metaphors do not merely actualize a potential connotation, but establish it "as a staple one"; and further, "some of [the object's] relevant properties can be given a new status as elements of verbal meaning."[12]

However, to speak of properties of *things* (or *objects*), which are supposed not yet to have been signified, is to admit that the new, emergent meaning is not drawn from anywhere, at least not from anywhere in language (the property is an implication of things, not of words). To say that a new metaphor is not drawn from anywhere is to recognize it for what it is: namely, a

[9] Beardsley, *Aesthetics*, 138. – Ricoeur's note.
[10] Beardsley, "The Metaphorical Twist," 302. – Ricoeur's note
[11] Ibid. – Ricoeur's note.
[12] Ibid. – Ricoeur's note.

momentary creation of language, a semantic innovation which does not have a status in the language as something already established, whether as a designation or as a connotation.

It may be asked how can we speak of a semantic innovation, a semantic event, as a meaning capable of being identified and reidentified (that was the first criterion of discourse stated above). Only one answer remains possible: it is necessary to take the viewpoint of the hearer or the reader and to treat the novelty of the emergent meaning as the counterpart, on the author's side, of a construction on the side of the reader. Thus the process of explanation is the only access to the process of creation.

If we do not take this path, we do not really free ourselves from the theory of substitution; instead of substituting a literal meaning restored by paraphrase of the metaphorical expression, we substitute the system of connotations and commonplaces. This task must remain a preparatory one, enabling literary criticism to be reconnected to a psychology and sociology. The decisive moment of explanation is the construction of a network of inter- actions that constitutes the context as actual and unique. In so doing, we direct our attention toward the semantic event that is produced at the point of intersection between several semantic fields. This construction is the means by which all of the words taken together make sense. Then and only then, the "metaphori- cal twist" is both an event and a meaning, a meaningful event and an emergent meaning in language.

Such is the fundamental feature of explanation which makes metaphor a paradigm for the explanation of a literary work. We construct the meaning of a text in a manner similar to the way in which we make sense of all the terms of a metaphorical statement.

Why must we "construct" the meaning of a text? First, because it is written: in the asymmetrical relation between the text and the reader, one of the partners speaks for both. Bringing a text to language is always something other than hearing someone and listening to his speech. Reading resembles instead the perfor- mance of a musical piece regulated by the written notations of the score. For the text is an autonomous space of meaning that is no longer animated by the intention of its author; the autonomy of the text, deprived of this essential support, hands writing over to the sole interpretation of the reader.

A second reason is that the text is not only something written but is a work, that is, a singular totality. As a totality, the literary work cannot be reduced to a sequence of sentences that are individually intelligible; rather, it is an architecture of themes and purposes that can be constructed in several ways. The relation of part to whole is ineluctably circular. The presupposition of a certain whole precedes the discernment of a determinate arrangement of parts; and it is by constructing the details that we build up the whole. Moreover, as the notion of singular totality suggests, a text is a kind of individual, like an animal or a work of art. Its singularity can be regained, therefore, only by progressively rectifying the generic concepts that concern the class of texts, the literary genre, and the various structures that intersect in this singular text. In short, understanding a work involves the sort of judgment Kant explored in the third *Critique*.

What, then, can we say about this construction and this judgment? Here understanding a text, at the level of its articulation of sense, is strictly homologous to understanding a metaphorical statement. In both cases, it is a question of "making sense," of producing the best overall intelligibility from an apparently discordant diversity. In both cases, the construction takes the form of a wager or guess. As E. D. Hirsch says in *Validity in Interpretation*, there are no rules for making good guesses, but there are methods for validating our guesses.[13] This dialectic between guessing and validating is the realization at the textual level of the micro-dialectic at work in the resolution of the local enigmas of a text. In both cases, the procedures of validation have more affinity with a logic of probability than with a logic of empirical verification – more affinity, let us say, with a logic of uncertainty and qualitative probability. Validation, in this sense, is the concern of an argumentative discipline akin to the juridical procedures of legal interpretation.

We can now summarize the corresponding features that underlie the analogy between the explanation of metaphorical statements and that of a literary work as a whole. In both cases, the construction rests upon "clues" contained in the text itself. A clue serves as a guide for a specific construction, in that it contains

---

[13] E. D. Hirsch, *Validity in Interpretation* (New Haven: Yale University Press, 1967).

both a permission and a prohibition; it excludes unsuitable constructions and allows those which give more meaning to the same words. Second, in both cases, one construction can be said to be more probable than another, but not more truthful. The more probable is that which, on the one hand, takes account of the greatest number of facts furnished by the text, including its potential connotations, and on the other hand, offers a qualitatively better convergence between the features that it takes into account. A mediocre explanation can be called narrow or forced.

Here I agree with Beardsley when he says that a good explanation satisfies two principles: the principle of congruence and that of plenitude. Until now, we have in fact spoken about the principle of congruence. The principle of plentitude will provide us with a transition to the third part of this essay. The principle may be stated as follows: "All of the connotations that are suitable must be attributed; the poem means all that it can mean."[14] This principle leads us beyond a mere concern with "sense"; it already says something about reference, since it takes as a measure of plenitude the requirements stemming from an experience that asks to be said and to be equaled by the semantic density of the text. I shall say that the principle of plenitude is the corollary, at the level of meaning, of a principle of full expression that draws our expression in a quite different direction.

A quotation from Humboldt will lead us to the threshold of this new field of investigation: "Language as discourse (*Rede*) lies on the boundary between the expressible and the inexpressible. Its aim and its goal is to push back still further this boundary."[15]

Interpretation, in its proper sense, similarly lies on this frontier.

---

[14] Beardsley, *Aesthetics*, 144.

[15] Pierre Caussat, who did the French translation of Humboldt's *Introduction à l'oeuvre sur le Kavi* at Ricoeur's suggestion, believes Ricoeur was citing this passage from memory, or drawing on a free translation, which we have not been able to identify. We thank him for his help on this matter. [In English, see Wilhelm von Humboldt, *On Language: On the Diversity of Human Language Construction and Its Influence on the Mental Development of the Human Species*, ed. Michael Losonsky, trans. Peter Heath (Cambridge: Cambridge University Press, 1999). – trans.]

From Text to Metaphor: Interpretation

At the level of interpretation properly speaking, understanding the text provides the key to understanding metaphor.

Why? Because certain features of discourse begin to play an explicit role only when discourse takes the form of a literary *work*. These features are the very ones that we have placed under the heading of reference and self-reference. It will be recalled that I opposed reference to sense, saying that sense is the "what" and reference the "about what" of discourse. Of course, these two features can be recognized in the smallest units of language as discourse, namely, in sentences. The sentence is about a situation that it expresses, and it refers back to its speaker by means of the specific procedures that we have enumerated. But reference and self-reference do not give rise to perplexing problems so long as discourse has not become a text and has not taken the form of a work. What are these problems?

Let us begin once again from the difference between written and spoken languages. In spoken language, that to which a dialogue ultimately refers is the situation common to the inter-locutors, that is, the aspects of reality that can be shown or pointed to; we then say that the reference is "ostensive." In written language, the reference is no longer ostensive; poems, essays, works of fiction speak of things, events, states of affairs and characters that are evoked but which are not there. And yet literary texts are about something. About what? I do not hesitate to say: about a world, which is the world of that work. Far from saying that the text is without a world, I shall say that only now does man have a world and not merely a situation, a *Welt* and not merely an *Umwelt*. In the same way that the text frees its meaning from the tutelage of mental intention, so too it frees its reference from the limits of ostensive reference. For us, the world is the totality of references opened up by texts. Thus we speak of the "world" of ancient Greece, not to indicate what the situations were for those who experienced them, but to designate the non-situational references that outlast the effacement of these original situations and which then offer themselves as possible modes of being, as possible symbolic dimensions of our being in the world.

The nature of reference in the context of literary works has an important consequence for the concept of interpretation. It implies that the meaning of a text lies not behind the text but in front of it. The meaning is not something hidden but something disclosed. What gives rise to understanding is that which points toward a possible world, by means of the non-ostensive references of the text. Texts speak of possible worlds and possible ways of orientating oneself in these worlds. In this way, disclosure plays the equivalent role for written texts as ostensive reference plays in spoken language. Interpretation thus becomes the apprehension of the proposed worlds that are opened up by the non-ostensive reference of the text.

This concept of interpretation expresses a decisive shift of emphasis with respect to the Romantic tradition of hermeneutics. In that tradition, the emphasis was placed on the ability of the hearer or reader to transfer him- or herself into the mental life of a speaker or writer. The emphasis, from now on, is less on the other as a mental entity than on the world that the work unfolds. To understand is to follow the dynamic of the work, its movement from what it says to that about which it speaks. Beyond my situation as reader, beyond the situation of the author, I offer myself to the possible mode of being-in-the-world that the text opens up and discloses to me. This is what Gadamer calls the "fusion of horizons" (*Horizontverschmelzung*) in historical knowledge.

The shift of emphasis from understanding the other to understanding the world of the work entails a corresponding shift in the conception of the "hermeneutical circle." For the thinkers of Romanticism, the latter term meant that the understanding of the text cannot be an objective procedure, in the sense of scientific objectivity, but that it necessarily implies a pre-understanding, expressing the way in which the reader already understands himself and his work. Hence a sort of circularity is produced between understanding the text and self-understanding. This, in condensed terms, is the principle of the hermeneutical circle. It is easy to see how thinkers trained in the tradition of logical empiricism could only reject, as utterly scandalous, the very idea of a hermeneutical circle and consider it to be an outrageous violation of all the canons of verifiability.

For my part, I do not wish to conceal the fact that the hermeneutical circle remains an unavoidable structure of interpretation.

An interpretation is not genuine unless it culminates in some form of appropriation (*Aneigung*), if by that term we understand the process by which one makes one's own (*eigen*) what was initially other or alien (*fremd*). But I believe that the hermeneutical circle is not correctly understood when it is presented, first, as a circle between two subjectivities, that of the reader and that of the author; and second, as the projection of the subjectivity of the reader into the reading itself.

Let us correct the first assumption so as also to be able to correct the second one.

What we make our own, what we appropriate for ourselves, is not an alien experience or a distant intention, but the horizon of a world toward which a work directs itself. The appropriation of the reference is no longer modeled on the fusion of consciousnesses, on empathy or sympathy. The emergence of the sense and the reference of a text in language is the coming to language of a world and not the recognition of another person. The second correction of the Romantic conception of interpretation results from this. If appropriation is the counterpart of disclosure, of a kind of opening, then the role of subjectivity must not be described in terms of projection. I would prefer to say that the reader understands himself in front of the text, in front of the world of the work. To understand oneself in front of a text is quite the contrary of projecting oneself and one's own beliefs and prejudices; it is to let the work and its world enlarge the horizon of the understanding I have of myself.

In this way, the hermeneutical circle is not repudiated but rather displaced from a subjectivistic level to an ontological one. The circle is between my mode of being – beyond the knowledge which I may have of it – and the mode opened up and disclosed by the text through the world of the work.

This is the model of interpretation that I now propose to transfer from texts, as long sequences of discourse, to the metaphor, understood as "a poem in miniature" (Beardsley). Of course, the metaphor is too short a discourse to unfold this dialectic between the disclosure of a world and the disclosure of oneself as faced with that world. Nevertheless, this dialectic does point to some features of metaphor that the modern theories cited so far do not seem to take into consideration, but which were not absent from the classical theory of metaphor.

Let us return to the theory of metaphor in Aristotle's *Poetics*.

Metaphor is only one of the "parts" (*merè*) of what Aristotle calls "diction" (*lexis*). As such, it belongs to a group of discursive procedures – using unusual words, coining new words, abbreviating or extending words – that all depart from the common (*kurion*) use of words. Now what constitutes the unity of *lexis*? Only its function in poetry. *Lexis*, in turn, is one of the "parts" (*merè*) of tragedy, taken as the paradigm of the poetic work. In the context of the *Poetics*, tragedy represents the level of the literary work as a whole. Tragedy, in the form of a poem, has sense and reference. In Aristotle's language, the "sense" of tragedy is secured by what he calls the "plot" (*muthos*). We understand the latter as the sense of tragedy because Aristotle constantly emphasizes its structural characteristic. The *muthos* must have unity and coherence; it must make of the represented actions something "whole and complete." The *muthos* is thus the principal "part" of tragedy, its "essence." All the other parts of tragedy – the "characters," the "thoughts," the "delivery," the "production" – are linked to the plot as means or conditions, or to the performance of tragedy as having a plot. We must draw the consequence that it is only in relation to the *muthos* of tragedy that its *lexis* takes on a sense, and the same thing applies to metaphor. There is no local meaning of metaphor outside of the regional meaning secured by the *muthos* of tragedy.

If metaphor is linked to the "sense" of tragedy by means of its *muthos*, it is also linked to the "reference" of tragedy in virtue of its general aim, which Aristotle calls *mimesis*.

Why do poets write tragedies, elaborate plots, use "unusual" words such as metaphors? Because tragedy itself is connected to a more fundamental human project, that of *imitating* human actions in a *poetic* way. With these two keywords – *mimesis* and *poiesis* – we reach the level that I have called the referential world of the work. Indeed, we may say that the Aristotelian concept of *mimesis* already encompasses all the paradoxes of reference. On the one hand, it expresses a world of human actions that is already there; tragedy is meant to express human reality, to express the tragedy of life. But on the other hand, *mimesis* does not mean the duplication of reality; *mimesis* is not a copy: *mimesis* is *poiesis*, that is, fabrication, construction, creation. Aristotle gives at least two indications of this creative dimension of *mimesis*.

First, the plot is an original, coherent construction that attests to the creative genius of the artist. Second, tragedy is an imitation of human actions that makes them appear better, higher, more noble than they are in reality. May we not say that *mimesis* is the Greek term for what I have called the non-ostensive reference of the literary work, or in other words, the Greek term for the disclosure of a world?

If this is right, we are now in a position to say something about the *power* of metaphor. I speak now of power and no longer of structure or even of process. The power of metaphor stems from its connection, internal to the poetic work, with three features: first, with the procedures of *lexis*; second, with the *plot*, which is the essence of the work, its immanent sense; and, third, with the intentionality of the work taken as a whole, that is, with its intention to represent human actions as higher than they are in reality – and therein lies the *mimesis*. In this sense, the power of metaphor arises from the power of the poem as a totality.

Let us apply these remarks, borrowed from Aristotle's *Poetics*, to our own description of metaphor.

Could we say that the feature of metaphor that we have placed above all others – its nascent or emergent character – is linked to the function of poetry as the creative imitation of reality? Why should we invent new meanings, meanings that exist only in the instant of discourse, if it were not to serve the *poiesis* in the *mimesis*? If it is true that the poem creates a world, then it requires a language that preserves and expresses its creative power in specific contexts.

By taking the *poiesis* of the poem together with metaphor as emergent meaning, we can make sense of both of them at the same time, both poetry and metaphor.

This is how the theory of interpretation paves the way for an ultimate approximation of the power of metaphor. The priority given to the interpretation of the text at this final stage of my analysis does not mean that the relation between the two is not reciprocal.

The explanation of metaphor, as a local event in the text, contributes to the interpretation of the work as a whole. We may even say that if the interpretation of local metaphors is illuminated by the interpretation of the text as a whole and by disentangling the kind of world that the work projects, in return the interpretation of the poem taken as a whole is controlled by the explanation of the metaphor as a local phenomenon of the text.

As an example of this reciprocal relation between the regional and local aspects of the text, I shall venture to mention a possible connection, implicit in Aristotle's *Poetics*, between what he says about *mimesis* on the one hand and metaphor on the other. *Mimesis*, we have seen, makes human actions appear higher than they are in reality; but it is the function of metaphor to transpose the meanings of ordinary language by way of unusual uses. Is there not a mutual and profound affinity between the project of making human actions appear better than they are and the special procedure of metaphor that raises language above itself?

Let us express this relation in more general terms. Why should we draw new meanings from our language if we have nothing new to say, no new world to project? The creations of language would be devoid of meaning if they did not serve the general project of letting new worlds emerge by means of poetry.

Allow me to conclude in a way that will be consistent with a theory of interpretation that places the emphasis on "opening up a world." Our conclusion should also "open up" some new perspectives, but on what? Perhaps on the old problem of the imagination, which I have carefully put aside. Are we not ready to recognize in the power of imagination, no longer the faculty of deriving "images" from our sensory experience, but the capacity for letting new worlds shape our understanding of ourselves? This power will not be conveyed through images, but through the emergent meanings in our language. Imagination then has to be treated as a dimension of language. In this way, a new link might appear between imagination and metaphor. We shall, for the time being, refrain from entering this half-open door.

3

"Hermeneutical Logic"?

Can we speak of a hermeneutical logic?[1] In truth, to the best of my knowledge this term has been employed only by Hans Lipps in his *Untersuchungen zu einer hermeutischen Logik* [*Investigations Leading to a Hermeneutical Logic*] from 1938.[2] These investigations were cut off, first by Lipps's premature death, but above all owing to the blow that Heidegger's radicalization of hermeneutics represented, which made Lipps appear too closely tied to Georg Misch's *Lebensphilosophie* [philosophy of "life"] from which philosophical hermeneutics after Heidegger distanced itself in a particularly decisive manner. Yet a certain type of return to Lipps is worth considering, in that his work does have some relation to the general tendency of post-Heideggerian hermeneutics

[1] This essay was originally presented as a lecture to the Institut international de philosophie in 1978, then printed in French in Guttorm Fløistad, ed., *Contemporary Philosophy: A New Survey*, vol. 1: *Philosophy of Language* (The Hague: Martinus Nijhoff, 1981), 179–223.

[2] Hans Lipps, *Untersuchungen zu einer hermeneutischen Logik* (Frankfurt: Klostermann, 1938, 1959). An extract appears in Hans-Georg Gadamer and Gottfried Boehm, eds, *Seminar: Philosphische Hermeneutik* (Frankfurt: Suhrkamp, 1976), 286–316. Otto F. Bollnow spells out Lipps's relation to the "philosophy of life" of Georg Misch in "Zum Begriff der hermeneutischen Logik," in Otto Pöggeler, ed., *Hermeneutische Philosophie: Zehn Aufsätze* (Munich: Nymphenburger, 1972), 100–22. – Ricoeur's note.

in its reflections on the conditions of possibility of its own discourse, and thus in the way it situates itself in relation to the logical preoccupations that have taken center stage in some other currents of contemporary philosophy. My essay will devote itself, particularly in the sections on the hermeneutical claim to universality and the reply from hermeneutics, to this twofold effort of hermeneutic philosophy in the past few years to reflect upon its epistemological status. However, before that I shall recall how the problem created by Heidegger and then developed by Gadamer has been posed.

An Anti-Logical Radicalization?

At first glance, Heidegger's radicalization of hermeneutics marks the taking of a distance from the epistemological questions that dominated the period of Dilthey's influence.[3] With Dilthey, it was still possible to situate hermeneutics at the level of the epistemological discussion, without locking it up there. Three things were at issue. First of all, it was a question of defending the autonomy of the human sciences in relation to the natural sciences; then to establish the difference between understanding, their principal way of proceeding, and explanation as it was used in the natural sciences; finally, there was the question of grounding this epistemological difference in a fundamental property of mental life, namely, the power of a subject to transport itself into an alien psychological life. Beyond question therefore, Dilthey's hermeneutics was inscribed in the epistemological debate in that it was the very "scientificity" of the hermeneutical sciences that was at

[3] Besides the recent publication of Heidegger's unpublished work and the texts now appearing in his *Gesamtausgabe* (Frankfurt: Kosterman, 1975–), see the following works devoted to an interpretation of his philosophy: Otto Pöggler, ed., *Heidegger: Perspektiven zur Deutung seines Werkes* (Cologne/Berlin: Athenäum, 1969); Pöggler, ed., *Hermeneutische Philosophie: Zehn Aufsätze* (Munich: Nymphenberger, 1972); Ernst Tugenhat, *Der Wahrheitsbegriff bei Husserl und Heidegger* (Berlin: Walter de Gruyter, 1967); Hans-Georg Gadamer, "Martin Heidegger und die Marburger Theologie," in *Heidegger: Perspektiven*; Joseph J. Kockelmans, ed. *On Heidegger and Language* (Evanston: Northwestern University Press, 1972). – Ricoeur's note.

stake as regards the three levels that determined their field, established their principle way of proceeding, and grounded their specificity. This latter question indicated a passage from epistemology in the strict sense of the term to a Kantian-style transcendental interrogation that subordinated methodological questions to the investigating of their conditions of possibility.

Heidegger's hermeneutical philosophy appeared to break precisely with this kind of questioning. It did so, again, in a threefold way. First of all, it was not the justification of the specificity of the human sciences that his philosophy concerned itself with, at least not directly. His question was an ontological one: what being are we, we who ask ourselves the question of being? Already with the introduction to *Being and Time* [in 1927], the non-epistemological radicality of his question is clear.[4] If we inquire first of all about the being we ourselves are – *Dasein* – this is because it is the privileged site for this fundamental question. It is merely as "preparatory" that the analytic of Dasein takes center stage. The question of meaning – the hermeneutical question par excellence – is the question of the meaning of being. In this way, a question whose origin was Aristotelian supplants a Kantian one. The second break: the question of understanding – implied in the question of the meaning of being – is not itself an epistemological question, at least not initially. Understanding is a distinctive feature of the being we are, a property of Dasein as "being-in-the-world." Interpretation therefore is simply the development of understanding, inasmuch as understanding something *as* something is already to interpret it. This interpretation, in turn, gets articulated in a discourse that determines and makes explicit the articulations of a situation and an understanding that were initially bound to a more fundamental level than such discourse. The claim to begin with discourse expressed through propositions and therefore to place oneself within an *apophantic logos* is the most basic misunderstanding against which hermeneutics reacts. The first setting for any articulation is being-in-the-world itself. And it is the connection between situation–understanding–interpretation and discourse that underlies every investigation at a purely propositional level. Third break: It is not in terms of

[4] Martin Heidegger, *Being and Time*, trans. John Macquarrie and Edward Robinson (New York: Harper and Brothers, 1962).

conditions of possibility that the problem of understanding finally comes down to. For a Kantian perspective, to ask about conditions of possibility means referring to an epistemological subject that carries categories that govern the objectivity of any object. But what the analytic of Dasein lays bare is not a subject of knowledge, but a thrown-projecting being. Before the cognitive relation between subject and object, therefore, understanding is implied in this ontological structure of thrown-being and anticipation. This mode of being is better designated as "care" than as knowledge. The question of being, which I have said precedes any investigation into the human sciences, is included in this care, as a kind of ontological pre-understanding.

This subordination of epistemology to ontology reaches its decisive point when the methodology of the human sciences finds itself supplanted by an interrogation into the historicity of Dasein: before history has an object and a method, we are historical through and through.

This – broadly speaking – is the anti-epistemological and anti-logical motivation for Heidegger's radicalization of hermeneutics in *Sein und Zeit*.

Yet, in the post-Heideggerian phase that interests us here, this radicalized hermeneutics must not escape questioning of an epistemological kind, once one can do it and once we have inquired into the conditions of possibility of hermeneutical discourse and situated it in relation to those philosophies making claims based on logic and epistemology, particularly as in contemporary analytic philosophy.

We must admit that this second-degree reflection is hardly indicated in *Sein und Zeit*. Still we do find a few indications of it in all the passages where the type of hermeneutical truth is at issue. For example, we read in §7 that hermeneutics is a kind of phenomenology. But whoever says phenomenology also says: *logos* of what shows itself. What we must do therefore is to situate this hermeneutic logos in relation to the apophantic logos, that of propositional logic. If this apophantic logos is articulated first of all in the proposition that says something about something, what relation exists between this "about" and the hermeneutic "about" or *as* that, as already stated, constitutes the moment of interpretation, which develops and articulates the moment of understanding (see *Sein und Zeit* §32 and §33)? In this way, a new concept of truth is called for, which is not defined by the characteristics of the proposition, but by the capacity for unveiling implied in the relation between situation and under-standing. Yet, at the same time, hermeneutic philosophy also makes a truth claim that has to be measured against the apophan-tic, that is, the propositional truth claim.

There is another way in which hermeneutic philosophy has to ask an epistemological question of itself. The characterization of Dasein brings into play a type of discourse called an *existential analytic*. Two things are implied by this expression. On the one hand, far from being a return to the ineffable and the irrational, as is sometimes mistakenly said, hermeneutic philosophy is an analytic in that it proceeds by making distinctions, determina-tions, and finding relationships (hence the frequent occurrence of the term "structure" in *Sein und Zeit* and the strong didactic char-acter in the way the work is constructed). On the other hand, this analytic is an existential one in that it articulates quasi-categories – being-in-the-world, situation, understanding, and so on – that are to Dasein what categories in analytic philosophy are to things. This distinction between "existentials" and categories is certainly based on an ontological distinction between different modes of being: the being we are – Dasein, which alone ex-ists – and "things" which are things either present-to-hand (*vorhandene*) or ready-to-hand (*zuhandene*). This distinction between modes of being comes to language and discourse precisely as a categorial difference. In this sense, hermeneutics cannot avoid the Kantian question of the conditions of possibility of its own discourse.

It comes back to this question also in a third way: However radical the hermeneutical interrogation coming from Heidegger may be, it cannot eliminate the fact that hermeneutics is born out of a problematic that comes from the human sciences. It is in fact this problematic for which it is a radicalization. In this way, the confrontation with Dilthey's hermeneutics is an integral part of the hermeneutical enterprise. Its claim to found the human sci-ences remains the undeniable epistemological component of hermeneutical discourse, at least in the third sense I earlier attached to Dilthey's epistemology. In fact, many analyses in *Sein und Zeit* point in this direction without completely taking them up. For example, the derivation of the problematic of the histori-cal sciences starting from the ontology of historicity is sketched out in the analyses that show in what way historicity, originarily oriented toward the future, turns toward the past through the mediation of "repetition," and how one passes from the process of temporalization (*Zeitlichkeit*), inherent in the dialectic of situation and understanding, to "being-in time" (*Innerzeitlichkeit*), which implies the standard for and the references to public "dating." But we do not go any further in the derivation of the most far-removed conditions of historical knowledge. There is no conceptual construction of the categories that would allow us to take this derivation for anything other than the allegation of the ontological priority of historicity in relation to the discipline that studies history. Or, if one would prefer that it be put another way, we do not see in what way the conditions of possibility of the ontological inquiry are also the conditions of possibility of objective historical knowledge. It seems as if with Heidegger we move toward the foundation, but without the "second navigation" – to speak like Plato – that would bring us back toward the epistemology of the human sciences.

We need to mention another important contribution of *Sein und Zeit* to the epistemology of the human sciences. It has less to do with the historical character of these disciplines than with their textual status. Older forms of hermeneutics always argued about the circle – the well-known hermeneutical circle – thanks to which the interpreter's anticipations of meaning are an integral part of the meaning to be interpreted. To understand a text, it must already have been pre-understood. And this pre-understanding cannot be eliminated, except at the cost of breaking the contract between the interpreting and the interpreted by means of which the interpreter reaches the intended meanings of the text. From an epistemological point of view, this implication of the interpreter in the thing interpreted must appear as a weakness, a subjectivist flaw, when compared to the objectivity that the scientific ideal requires. Heidegger justifies the hermeneutic circle by showing that its apparent epistemological weakness stems from its real ontological strength. The most originary circle is the one that exists in each case between pre-understanding and the worldly situation to be interpreted. This is not a vicious circle; it constitutes the positive condition of the most originary kind of knowledge. This argument is telling; it is part of the general strategy of *Sein und Zeit*, which is to bring questions of method back to their ontological roots. But we do not see how to return from this ground to the properly epistemological difficulties having to do with the interpretation of texts. In particular, the subordination of the epistemological circle to the ontological one does not allow us to make a choice between different ways of comporting ourselves in relation to a text. Does the ontologizing of the hermeneutical problem imply the complete liquidation of its psychologization in Dilthey? In particular, must we abandon every claim to measure the meaning of the text in terms of the author's intention? Must we stop trying to understand an author better than he understood himself? Or again, must we abandon the idea of reaching the intended meaning of a text, of rendering ourselves contemporary with it (whether this be with the meaning of the text or the author's meaning)? Must we stop defining hermeneutics as the struggle against misunderstanding, through appropriation of what is alien to us? As the struggle against distance in space and time? As the reproduction of an originary production? The return to foundations in Heidegger is so radical that the derived questions are in a way lost from sight, as though they had become inessential, even irrelevant, through this return to a ground. Yet it was not on the basis of hermeneutic philosophy that these questions were posed in the past by biblical exegesis, by classical philology, by jurisprudence, and are still posed by literary hermeneutics, which I shall return to below. What is more, it is through its capacity to return to these questions that the claim of hermeneutics to be a fundamental discipline, in the proper sense of this term, is to be measured.

Truth and/or Method?

The same kind of questions are raised by Gadamer's major work, *Truth and Method*, which constitutes the second link between the hermeneutics of the human sciences coming from Dilthey and this inquiry into the epistemological condition of hermeneutics.[5]

---

[5] Hans-Georg Gadamer, *Wahrheit und Methode: Grundzüge einer philosophischen Hemeneutik* (Tübingen: Mohr/Siebeck, 1960, ²1965, ³1967); *Truth and Method*, second, revised edition, trans. Joel Weinsheimer and Donald G. Marshall (New York: Crossroad, 1991). I will also take note of the important introductions to the second and third editions. See also Gadamer, *Kleine Schriften I und II* (Tübingen: Mohr/Siebeck, 1967). – Ricoeur's note.

In many ways Gadamer's title invites us to read it as an alternative: truth *or* method. This is probably how readers trained in the tradition of analytic philosophy would read it.

The initial experience from which the work begins – the place from which it speaks – is the scandal constituted, for modern consciousness, by the kind of alienating (*Verfremdung*) distance that, more than being just a feeling or emotion, is the ontological condition that supports objective research in the human sciences. The methodology of these sciences ineluctably implies setting things at a distance, which in turn presupposes the destruction of the primordial relation of belonging to – *Zugehörigkeit* – without which no relation to an object would exist. Gadamer pursues this argument over alienating distance and an experience of belonging-to in three spheres into which, he says, hermeneutical experience can be divided: an aesthetic sphere, a historical sphere, and a linguistic sphere. In the aesthetic sphere, the experience of being grasped by a work of art is what always precedes and makes possible that critical exercise of judgment, for which Kant provided a theory in terms of the judgment of taste. In the historical sphere, it is the consciousness of being borne by traditions that makes possible the exercise of a historical methodology at the level of the human and social sciences. Finally, in the sphere of language, which in a way runs through the two preceding spheres, that the things said by the great creators of discourse and the things talked about belong together, precedes and makes possible every instrumental reduction of language and every claim to dominate the structures of the text of our culture technically. In this sense, a single thesis runs through the three parts of *Truth and Method*.

The argument about the *Geisteswissenschaften* therefore does not constitute the sole anchorage for philosophical hermeneutics. On the contrary, the entry into the problematic through aesthetics is irreplaceable. It is where hermeneutics finds in common consciousness its best handhold for shattering the claim by judging consciousness to set itself up as the arbiter of taste and master of meaning. Thanks to this first breakthrough, philosophical hermeneutics can bring about a second breakthrough, at the level of historical experience, and in this way get back together again with what was, chronologically speaking, its initial starting point. In this way, the universality claimed by hermeneutics in the debate we shall consider later, between hermeneutics and the critique of ideologies, does not exclude but instead requires this multiplicity of concrete anchoring points. But it is not a matter of indifference that Gadamer should have set aside as less important a reflection on "being toward the text" (*Sein zum Text*) wherein he sees the danger of a reduction of hermeneutic experience to translation, set up as the linguistic model of human behavior in regard to the world.

If we now concentrate on the second part of *Wahrheit und Methode*, the three points where Gadamer's rejection of methodology is clearest and which his critics have most dwelt upon are the rehabilitation of prejudice, tradition, and authority; the notion of *Wirkungsgeschichte* [history as having an effect]; and that of the "fusion of horizons." These are also the three points where it will be possible to tie a less anti-methodological reading of *Wahrheit und Methode* and to give it a less disjunctive interpretation.

It was surely as a kind of provocation that Gadamer undertook his plea in favor of prejudice. Prejudice is a category from the *Aufklärung* [the Enlightenment]. It is what one must get rid of in order "to dare to think" – *sapere aude!*, exclaimed Kant – and to accede to the age of "adulthood." Yet prejudice is so unequivocally negative only for a critical philosophy, a philosophy of judgment. In turn, what sets up judgment as a court of judgment is a philosophy that makes objectivity, whose model is provided by the sciences, the measure of knowledge. Along with Heidegger, we need to consider that no subject of knowledge reaches a domain of knowledge unless it has first projected onto this domain a pre-understanding that assures its familiarity with this domain. Yet this pre-understanding is not entirely transparent to reflection. No transcendental subject ever attains perfect mastery of it. This is why prejudice is merely the projection on the plane of judgment of a fundamental hermeneutical category: tradition. Human beings discover their finitude in the fact that they first find themselves amid traditions.[6] Tradition is positively the expression of the finite historical character of self-understanding for human beings. The third term of the trilogy – prejudice, tradition, authority – only makes explicit this role of tradition in terms of its

[6] See Gadamer, *Truth and Method*, "The Rehabilitation of Authority and Tradition," 277–85.

efficacity. But its significance is hidden from us by the prejudice stemming from the *Aufklärung* for which authority is a synonym for domination, in the sense of violence, and submission to authority is a synonym for blind obedience.

The epistemological consequence of this plea is that the *Geisteswissenschaften* – with history the first among them – are built upon the prior ground of the transmission and reception of traditions. *Forschung* – inquiry – does not escape the historical consciousness of those who live and make history. It is starting from a tradition that calls for inquiry that history poses "meaningful" questions to the past. A contract is enacted between the action of history and historical investigation from which no critical consciousness can release itself, except at the cost of making its own research "senseless."

This "historical" (*geschichtlich*) condition of history (*Historie*) is expressed through the concept of *Wirkungsgeschichte* (literally: history of effects). This category no longer comes from historical methodology, but from the reflective consciousness of methodology. It is the consciousness of beings exposed to history and its action, in a way where one cannot objectify this action on them, because this efficacity is part of its meaning as a historical phenomenon. This consciousness of effects has a negative and a positive meaning. Negatively, it excludes any view from above that would allow us to master our view of the whole set of effects of the past on us; historical being is what does not pass over into absolute knowledge. Here the philosophy of hermeneutics, in contrast to any Hegelian absorption into absolute knowledge, is a philosophy of finitude. Positively, it must be said that the concept of effective history mediates our relation to the past. Starting from this mediation, something is significant, interesting, important, memorable; in short, worthy of being related through a historical inquiry.

That effective history in no way signifies that we are prisoners of the past is attested to by the third key concept, that of a "fusion of horizons." The concept of a "horizon" completes and corrects that of a "situation." The horizon is what a point of view picks out. Talk of a fusion of horizons means admitting, along with Dilthey's hermeneutics, that it is always possible to transfer oneself into another's point of view. But this transfer is not a psychological riddle. If it is possible to enter into a dialectic of points of view, this is because, in the tension between self and other, a prior agreement about the thing itself leads inquiry to an actual agreement. But, in turn, this prior agreement cannot be transformed into objective knowledge that would abolish the alterity of points of view, by placing all points of view at a distance. Then no one would have anything more to say in this dialogue, no one could bring anything new to the discussion. We do not exist in closed horizons or in a unique horizon with an objective-empirical or dialectical-speculative character. The idea of a "fusion of horizons" like that of "effective history" has both negative and positive implications. It signifies negatively the refusal of any objectifying closure or any speculative *Aufhebung* [sublation]. It signifies positively that it is by starting from a "fusion of horizons," and the prior agreement about the thing itself that upholds it, that the transfer to another point of view, to another culture, which is the basis for historical knowledge, is possible.

What does all this have to say about the relation between truth and method? Let us say first, speaking generally, that the relation between truth and method is not one of simple opposition or mutual exclusion. This would be the case if historical understanding were opposed on the same plane as scientific explanation. In this regard, Rudiger Bubner is right to set us on guard against an interpretation of *Wahrheit und Methode* that would come down purely and simply to the methodological dichotomy that Dilthey was not able to overcome.[7] Hermeneutic philosophy is not anti-epistemological, but a reflection on the non-epistemological conditions of epistemology. The three categories we have reviewed indicate the unsurpassable conditions for the constitution of a meaningful space in which something can have the value of a historical object.

[7] Rudiger Bubner, "Über die wissenschaftstheoretische Rolle der Hermeneutik," in *Dialektik und Wissenschaft* (Suhrkamp, 1973), 89–111. According to this author, only a transcendental interpretation of hermeneutics can deal with the attacks directed against it by Hans Albert in his *Treatise on Critical Reason*, trans. Mary Varney Rorty (Princeton: Princeton University Press, 1985). See also, Bubner, "Transzendentale Hermeneutik?" in Roland Simon-Schäfer, and Walter Ch. Zimmerli, eds, *Wissenschaftstheorie der Geisteswissenschaften* (Hamburg: Hoffman und Campe, 1975), 56–70. – Ricoeur's note.

On the basis of this general remark, it is possible to give *Wahrheit und Methode* a more dialectical interpretation between the two terms than previously. Each of the three historical categories indicates the place of an appropriate critical moment that assures the mediation between hermeneutics and the objective human sciences.

The rehabilitation of prejudice does not signify submission to every tradition, but only the impossibility of removing oneself from the condition for historical transmission. The counterpart to the authority of tradition, is the "recognition (*Anerkennung*) of its superiority": authority, says *Wahrheit und Methode*, "has nothing to do with blind obedience to commands but rather with knowledge."[8] What, in the last instance, has authority, is the tradition starting from which we inquire. To admit this is not to sacrifice reason. For the "preservation" (*Bewahrung*) of a cultural heritage does not happen apart from some criticism, hence without a permanent debate between a spirit of innovation and a spirit of conservation. In this regard, Gadamer names "application" (*Anwendung*) the operation that plays in regard to tradition in general the role verification plays in regard to a scientific hypothesis. It is juridical hermeneutics that has best understood its importance: application marks out the open space in which the judge is distinguished from the legislator. Application also gets its *lettres de noblesse* from ancient rhetoric, which is addressed to an audience, whose passions it acknowledges, in order either to convince or persuade it. This fundamental category attests that the art of understanding is not complete without a critical actualization of meaning in the conditions of a new cultural situation.

The category of effective history also has a critical counterpart – namely, the concept of "*historical distance.*" Distance is first of all a fact, taking a distance is something more than this: it is a methodological move. The history of effects or of efficacity takes place precisely under the condition of distance in the twofold sense of a passive being at a distance and an active taking of a distance. In this way, it becomes the proximity of what is far off. The methodological illusion begins when we imagine that such distance puts an end to our complicity with the past and creates a situation comparable to objectivity in the natural sciences. The paradox of the alterity of the past stems precisely from the fact

[8] Gadamer, *Truth and Method*, 279.

that effective history is efficacity at a distance. Alienating distanciation begins when the moment of objectification is abstracted from its concrete site, that is, from the historian's belonging to the history that he undertakes to investigate.

As for the historical category of a "fusion of horizons," whose place I have emphasized in relation to any speculative *Aufhebung* or inclusion into objective knowledge, it too finds its critical complement in the structure of language developed in the third part of *Warheit und Methode*. In effect, all understanding of the world there appears conditioned by a *common linguistic practice*. But if this language-based community has to be subtracted from the objectification of language into a system of manipulable signs, it does not signify that the prior agreement about the thing itself, referred to earlier, implies an already given actual agreement (here too Bubner sets us on guard against any confusion between the presupposed agreement and any actual consensus whatsoever).[9] The only "logic" appropriate to the fusion of horizons is dialectic; that is, in the original sense of the term, the art of *questions and answers*. The epistemology of hermeneutics leads to this art of dialogue. It marks the inclusion of the critical moment of the question into the hermeneutics of understanding carried by the language-based community.

The Hermeneutic Claim to Universality Called into Question

These first mentions of inclusion of a critical moment in the overall process of understanding become more precise thanks to the argument over hermeneutics' claim to universality. The epistemological battle regarding hermeneutics crystallized around a precise point: what about its claim to universality?[10]

---

[9] Bubner, "Über die wissenschaftstheoretische Rolle der Hermeneutik," 97.

[10] Details regarding this debate can be found in Jürgen Habermas et al., *Hermeneutik und Ideologiekritik* (Frankfurt: Suhrkamp, 1971). See also Emilio Betti, *Allgemeine Auslegungslehre als Methode der Geisteswissenschaften* (Frankfurt: Mohr/Siebeck, 1955), the German translation of his *Teoria generale della interpretazione* (Milan: A. Giuffrè, 1955). – Ricoeur's note.

There is an argument because sometimes hermeneutics claims to govern all scientificity, inasmuch as all objective knowledge is rooted in a linguistic understanding of the world that precedes it; sometimes it seems to limit itself to the role of a *Kunstlehre* [theory of interpretation] for some group of sciences, those that the nineteenth century came to call the *Geisteswissenshaften.* In the first case, there can be no doubt about universality. It expresses the subordination of any explanation to a prior ground of understanding; on the other hand, the scientificity of this understanding is not certain. In the second case, the scientificity of hermeneutics is easier to justify within the framework of an epistemology of the human sciences, but its universality becomes doubtful, inasmuch as explanation falls outside understanding.

Two contributions in this regard – which actually are close to each other – are worth considering here, that of Karl-Otto Apel and that of Jürgen Habermas. They both tend to put the accent on the scientificity of hermeneutics to the exclusion of its universality and in this way lead to situating hermeneutics in a much broader "scientific" setting.

Schematically Habermas's critique [of the proposed universality of hermeneutics] can be summed up as follows.[11] Whereas Gadamer borrows from philosophical Romanticism the rehabilitation of prejudice and derives from the Heideggeran notion of pre-understanding his concept of effective historical consciousness, Habermas develops a concept of "interest" stemming from

---

[11] Jürgen Habermas, *On the Logic of the Social Sciences,* trans. Shierry Weber Nicholsen and Jerry A. Stark (Cambridge, MA: MIT Press, 1988); "A Review of Gadamer's *Truth and Method,*" in Gayle Ormiston and Alan D. Schrift, eds, *The Hermeneutic Tradition: From Ast to Ricoeur* (Albany: State University of New York Press, 1990), 213–44; "The Hermeneutic Claim to Universality," ibid., 245–72; *Knowledge and Human Interests,* trans. Jeremy J. Shapiro (Boston: Beacon Press, 1971); *Theory and Practice,* trans. John Viertel (Boston: Beacon Press, 1973); *Toward a Rational Society: Student Protest, Science, and Politics,* trans. Jeremy J. Shapiro (Boston: Beacon Press, 1970), 50–122; "Vorbereitende Bemerkungen zu einer Theorie der Kommunikativen Kompetenz," in Jürgen Habermas and Nicholas Luhmann, *Theorie der Gesellschaft oder Sozialtechnologie?* (Frankfurt: Surhkamp, 1971), 101–42. – Ricoeur's note

the Marxist critique of ideologies, itself interpreted in light of Lukács's *History and Class Consciousness* and the work of the Frankfurt School.[12] It is true that Habermas stands as far removed from Marxism as Gadamer does from German Romanticism. For the Marxist monistic concept of production, Habermas substitutes a pluralism of interests, where each one governs, in an a priori anthropological way, a scientific domain. An interest does so in the sense that the signification of possible statements in a sphere of objects is predetermined and prescribed by this interest. For example, to the technical or instrumental interest, defined as a "knowledge-constitutive interest in possible technical control," corresponds the sphere of empirical-analytic statements.[13] To the practical interest for interhuman communication correspond the historical-hermeneutic sciences; the signification of propositions produced in this domain does not proceed from a possible prediction and technical exploitation, but from the understanding of meaning; this understanding takes place through the channel of interpreting messages exchanged in ordinary language, by means of the interpretation of texts transmitted by tradition, and finally thanks to the internalization of norms that institutionalize social roles. The discussion of these two interests contains what is essentially Habermas's critique of Marx, who is accused of having confused the technical and the practical planes and of having reduced to positivism the critique of the conditions of possibility of human action, stemming from Kant, Fichte, and the left Hegelians. But it is the distinction between the interest in communication and a third interest, called an *interest in emancipation*, that marks the opposition to Gadamer. This third interest shifts the center of discussion, from the historical-hermeneutic sciences toward the critical social sciences, to which belong, essentially, the critique of ideologies and psychoanalysis. In this pair, the critique of ideologies provides the field of application, namely, bundles of systematically distorted interhuman communication; psychoanalysis [provides] the model of explanation, namely, the

[12] Georg Lukács, *History and Class Consciousness: Studies in Marxist Dialectics*, trans. Rodney Livingstone (Cambridge, MA: MIT Press, 1971).
[13] Habermas, *Knowledge and Human Interests*, 135.

quasi-objectification of processes whose opacity makes them inaccessible to a simple explanation in terms of their implicit presuppositions. It is this detour through quasi-observation and quasi-explanation that indicates the limits of hermeneutic understanding. Indeed, it appears to be limited to the clarification of forms of misunderstanding themselves homogeneous with understanding, as in the tradition of Schleiermacher and Dilthey. That the quasi-observations finally unblock an enlarged and deepened self-understanding, this latter episode will below give rise to an assault on the claims made by a hermeneutics that sets itself up as a meta-critique and a critical philosophy that sets itself up as a meta-hermeneutic. But before turning to this ultimate confrontation, let us examine the differences more closely.

In distinguishing the interest in emancipation that guides the critical social sciences from the interest in communication that governs the historical-hermeneutical ones, Habermas makes the limited character of hermeneutics appear as bound to one group of sciences, the "traditional" ones. Yet the notion of tradition is ambiguous. For one thing, it designates the incontestable fact of the dependence of every present project on a transmitted and understood past. But it also designates frozen ideological forms of interhuman relationships. If these reifications of the social bond can be transformed only through critique, it is because the discourse in which they express themselves shows a dependence between, on the one hand, language, and on the other, the pair formed by labor and domination. Here, hermeneutics can be accused of a linguistic idealism, insofar as it ignores this relationship of the dependence of language on social forces that make discourse a site of systematic distortions irreducible to phenomena of misunderstanding that a more penetrating understanding would suffice to dissolve. Ideology, in effect, works behind the backs of social partners. This is why its dissolution requires the detour of explanatory procedures and not simply ones of understanding, bringing into play a theoretical apparatus, like that of the Freudian metapsychology, that cannot be derived from a simple extension of the spontaneous art of interpretation at work in ordinary discourse and conversation.

If therefore hermeneutics is epistemologically limited – limited to the group of hermeneutical sciences – it is because it is philosophically limited by its misunderstanding of the relation between language and violence, arising from the conflict of social forces. In this sense, the ideological phenomenon, considered in terms of its individual or collective variants, constitutes a limit experience for hermeneutics.

The conflict between hermeneutics and the critique of ideology has to be carried to a deeper level of radicality. For Habermas, the principal fault of Gadamer's hermeneutics is its having ontologized hermeneutics. By this, he means Gadamer's insistence on agreement, accord, as though the consensus that precedes us were somehow constitutive, given with being. Habermas can only look with mistrust on what to him appears to be the ontological hypostasizing of a rare experience, namely, the experience of being preceded in our happiest dialogues by agreement. But we cannot canonize this experience, making it the paradigm of communicative action. What prevents us from doing so is precisely the ideological phenomenon. If ideology were solely an internal obstacle to understanding, a misunderstanding that the mere exercise of questions and answers could reintegrate, then one could say that where there is misunderstanding, there is a prior agreement. Hence it is for a critique of ideologies to think in terms of anticipation what hermeneutics thinks of in terms of an assumed tradition. In other words, the critique of ideologies implies that what hermeneutics conceives of as existing at the origin of understanding be posited as a regulative *idea*, in front of us. This regulative idea is that of unlimited, unconstrained communication. The Kantian accent is clear here; the regulative idea is more what ought to be than what is, more anticipation than reminiscence. It is this idea that gives meaning to psychoanalytic or sociological critique; for there is desymbolization only for a project of resymbolization; and there is no project except in the revolutionary perspective of an end to violence. An eschatology of non-violence thus constitutes the final philosophical horizon of a critique of ideologies. This eschatology, close to that of Ernst Bloch, takes the place held by the ontology of linguistic agreement in a hermeneutic of traditions.[14]

Karl-Otto Apel situates his evaluation of hermeneutics inside a larger project that would be to restore to the *Wissenschaftslehre*

---

[14] Ernst Bloch, *The Principle of Hope*, trans. Neville Plaice, Stephen Plaice, and Paul Knight (Cambridge, MA: MIT Press, 1986).

– which in German, has always meant more than "science" – its epistemic ground, without reducing it to a *"logic of science,"* in the sense of analytic philosophy.[15] This restoration can take place only through a reprise and broadening of the Kantian transcendental question, that is, through a reflection on the conditions of possibility of what, in a general manner, is taken as meaningful (*sinnvoll*). Second-order reflection on hermeneutics must therefore be transcendental, inasmuch as it bears on the condition of possibility of the discourse it articulates. But this reflection can be not carried out if it limits transcendental investigation to that region of meaning delimited by Kant under the rubric of objectivity and that he related to the unification of the manifold of experience under the categories of the understanding by a subject of pure knowledge. What Kant left out was a linguistic unification that precedes the categorial one. But this linguistic unification brings into play, beyond categorial understanding, a corporeal, technically mediated, commitment, and agreement of an intersubjective kind about the implicit norms of communication. This linguistic unification therefore requires more than an a priori of consciousness: a corporeal and social a priori; which, itself, brings into play the interests described and analyzed by Habermas, which have to be referred to a transcendental anthropology.

In this general perspective of an enlarged scientificity, Karl-Otto Apel develops two theses: the thesis of *complementarity* between what he calls *Scientistik* and hermeneutics, and the thesis of *mediation* of their rival claims brought about through the critique of ideologies.

The very idea of a complementarity between *Scientistik* and hermeneutics first implies that one reject the neopositivist program of a "unified science" and therefore that one take up anew the

---

[15] Karl-Otto Apel,"Scientistics, Hermeneutics, and the Critique of Ideology: Outline of a Theory of Science from a Cognitive-Anthropological Viewpoint," in *Towards a Transformation of Philosophy*, trans. Glyn Adey and David Frisby (London: Routledge and Kegan Paul, 1980), 46–76. See also Theodore Kisiel, "Zu einer Hermeneutik naturwissenschaftlicher Entdeckung," *Zeitschrift für allgemeine Wissenschaftstheorie* 2 (1971): 195–221; Gerard Radnitzky, *Contemporary Schools of Metascience* (New York: Humanities Press, 1970). – Ricoeur's note.

Diltheyian problem of the distinction between understanding and explanation.[16] Understanding, Apel argues, is not limited to a psychological operation extrinsic to logical operations; it does not have to do solely with a preparatory heuristic, as if science were to begin only with the positing of verifiable or falsifiable hypotheses. The justification of understanding as having its epistemological dimension rests partly on an argument like Dilthey's, namely, that in the hermeneutical sciences understanding makes up an integral part in the constitution of meaning. Hermeneutics finds here reinforcement inside the analytic camp, in the resistances posed by the epistemology of historical knowledge to the explanatory model proposed by Hempel and Popper.[17]

Yet it is interesting to see in what way this argument, stemming from an internal critique of analytic philosophy and borrowed from Dray, Danto, etc. is not just interpolated but truly integrated into the hermeneutic tradition whose origin lies with Dilthey.[18] It is from Heidegger and Gadamer that Apel gets the idea that all understanding brings into play a meaningful relationship between a project and a situation. This is why understanding remains the irreducible mode of intelligibility in history, inasmuch as a singular sequence of events draws its meaning from the relation between agents' intended meanings and a singular situation as they understood it.

In turn, this integration of a fragment of analytic philosophy into hermeneutics takes place thanks to a double inflection in hermeneutics itself. [First inflection:] on the one hand, one turns away from the question of the ontical–ontological difference, therefore from the question of being as being; and [on the other hand], places the accent almost exclusively on the linguistic

---

[16] Karl-Otto Apel, *Understanding and Explanation: A Transcendental-Pragmatic Perspective*, trans. Georgia Warnke (Cambridge, MA: MIT Press, 1984).
[17] Carl G. Hempel, "The Function of General Laws in History," *The Journal of Philosophy* 39 (1942): 35–48; Karl R. Popper, *The Logic of Scientific Discovery* (New York: Harper and Row, 1968).
[18] William Dray, *Laws and Explanation in History* (New York: Oxford University Press, 1957); Arthur Danto, *Analytical Philosophy of History* (New York: Cambridge University Press, 1965). – Ricoeur's note.

character of understanding the world. In this way, hermeneutics becomes essentially a *Sprachhermeneutik*.[19] This latter is tied to the presuppositions implicit in every formation of meaning, in the first rank, cultural transmissions. Second inflection of hermeneutics: the linguistic character of understanding the world according to Heidegger is linked to the Wittgensteinian theory of "language games" considered as "forms of life."[20]

We shall return below to this when we consider the argument between the two heritages of Wittgenstein and Heidegger. Two themes are essentially retained from the later Wittgenstein thanks to their analogy with those of *Sprachhermeneutik*: on the one hand, the idea that a linguistic articulation determines the limits of our world, on the other, the idea that this articulation is straightaway a public one. In this regard the Wittgensteinian critique of private language suppresses the Diltheyian, and in some respects Husserlian, problem of the passage from understanding that is in the first place subjective to an intersubjective understanding through transferring the intended meanings to others. Heidegger, Gadamer, and Wittgenstein meet here in an anti-psychologistic reaction.

The problem of historical knowledge, reinterpreted in this way in terms of a *Sprachhermeneutik*, itself inflected by its reception of Wittgenstein, then becomes: the understanding of reasons to act put in play by historical agents is irreducible to an explanation coming from a *Scientistik*. Historical knowledge is merely the rectification – in the double sense of being put to a critical test and a complication – of a language game that had already been played before history constituted itself as a science, namely, that of narrative practice within some cultural tradition.

However it is not this taking up again of the problem of historical knowledge in a hermeneutic perspective that best demonstrates the complementarity of *Scientistik* and hermeneutics. It is

[19] Karl-Otto Apel, "Sprache und Ordnung: Sprachanalytik versus Sprachhermeneutik," in Apel, *Transformation der Philosophie*, vol. 1 (Frankfurt: Suhrkamp, 1976), 167–96.
[20] Karl-Otto Apel, "Wittgenstein and Heidegger: Language Games and Life Forms," trans. Christopher Macann, in Apel, *From a Transcendental-Semiotic Point of View*, ed. Marianna Papstephanou (Manchester: Manchester University Press, 1998), 122–59.

on the very plane of scientific knowledge taken as a whole that the complementarity between objective explanation and intersubjective practical and linguistic agreement has to be shown. It must be said of all knowledge that it unites the two dimensions of *praxis*: the technical and the ethical dimensions. Indeed, the modern *praxis* most caught up in technology presupposes a prior agreement about the possibilities and norms of what is taken to be a meaningful being-in-the-world. Tradition is both the bond and the setting for this understanding. If therefore all knowledge implicitly presupposes the existence of a communication community, it is up to hermeneutics to thematize this presupposition. In this operation, the complementarity between *Scientistik* and hermeneutics gets attested to.

Why, though, appeal to a third discipline to do this? Here is where Apel and Habermas take their distance from Gadamer. For him, the existential commitment to a tradition is to be understood as an "application" that [mediates] between a past norm and the present situation. Through this application, its original force is restored to effective history in spite of any temporal distance. The model of interpretation has thus to be sought in the way a judge actualizes a norm in the act of judging.

Without denying that Gadamer is quite aware that hermeneutics will have nothing to say when a tradition has lost its force, therefore in a crisis situation where cultural transmission is threatened with a breakdown, Apel and Habermas see "application" more as a limitation on than as a concretizing of a hermeneutical project. One speaks of application only for religious texts that retain their authority, even if it be weakened, or for "classical" literary texts, those capable of a reactualization in any cultural situation, or juridical texts whose normative value remains uncontested. But this is not the *modern* relation to tradition. In this regard, the problem posed by non-European or non-American cultures is clearer and more radical than is our own. Reappropriation of the past here cannot be conceived of as application, but as having to pass through a radical doubt equivalent to an often painful distanciation. This means that we can no longer simply connect distanciation and methodological alienation. It is part of the modern condition in relation to tradition. In this sense, it is the same distanciation that makes possible appropriation *and* methodical abstraction. Apel readily concedes that it has become difficult today to hold together these two theses: on the one hand, in effect, it is necessary to say that there is no neutral point of view from which one can consider every tradition from a distance, except at the price of falling once again into the impasses of historicism. In this sense, the transmission of tradition remains the condition of access to any cultural object whatsoever, and, in this regard, with respect to the methodological illusion, hermeneutics functions to reveal its naivety. Yet, on the other hand, it is necessary to acknowledge that many traditions no longer speak to us, and that an immediate reappropriation of them is forbidden to us. What remains is our having to take advantage of distanciation, by practicing thanks to it a quasi-objectifying of transmitted contents, so as to reach a more mediate, more complex appropriation, for which in many cases we still do not have the key.

This quasi-objectifying is what is practiced in the critical social sciences, for which the model is psychoanalysis. It consists in treating cultural formations that have become alien to us as symptoms of *real* relations, of *material* structures belonging to another dimension than that of language. This is the case for the meaningful effects stemming from the relations between work and domination in capitalist industrial society. Discourse, work, and domination interweave networks of relationships whose opacity, whose non-transparency is not accidental but essential, not fragmentary but systematic. Hence a hermeneutics that bases itself on the capacity to make explicit the implicit, using only the force of discourse, can be accused of linguistic idealism. Such a hermeneutics runs up against what Apel considers to be the prolonging of natural history in cultural history. Without this non-transparency in principle, human beings would be able to equate their intended meanings and realize the ideal of mutual identification of Romantic hermeneutics. But until now they have not really been able to make their history; it happens for the most part behind their backs. This is why the integral reflective reprise of its meaning is impossible. The contingent factors of social existence can be analyzed only at the level of a quasi-objective explanation for which Freudian metapsychology is the model. At this level, the construction of models of explanation calls on a second-order terminology and conceptuality in which the actors do not participate. In return, hermeneutics does have the advantage when it recalls that this quasi-objectifying characteristic of the therapist's position is always a partially suspended communication whose final end is the reintegration of alienated meanings in a mediated, deepened self-understanding.

The consequence is that the quasi objective knowledge stemming from the therapeutic model cannot be absorbed into the objectivity of a *Scientistik*. If that were the case, the metalanguage of therapeutic explanation would allow it to found a technical mastery not just of the phenomena considered but over human beings themselves. This technical mastery would serve only to extend man's domination over man. The sole riposte to this danger is to subordinate the quasi-objectivity of the critical social sciences to a self-reflection within the framework of an ultimate self-understanding.

It is this mixed status of the critical social sciences that makes the critique of ideologies the mediating discipline between hermeneutics and *Scientistik*.

The Reply from Hermeneutics

The defense of the universality of hermeneutics was carried out at different levels by Gadamer, his disciples, and by those who, without identifying themselves with him, are close to him.[21]

---

[21] Hans-Georg Gadamer, "Rhetoric, Hermeneutics, and the Critique of Ideology," trans. J. Dibble, in Kurt Mueller-Vollmer, ed., *The Hermeneutic Reader* (Oxford: Blackwell, 1986), 274–92; "Reply to My Critics," in Ormiston and Schrift, eds, *The Hermeneutic Tradition*, 273–97. For a critique of Gadamer, see Wolfhart Pannenberg, "Hermeneutics and Universal History," trans. Paul J. Achtemeier, *Journal for Theology and the Church* 4 (1967): 122–52; Hirsch, *Validity in Interpretation*. Comparison should also be made to Lohmann's philosophy of language. For the general relationship between hermeneutics and the sciences, see Hans-Georg. Gadamer and Gottfried Boehm, eds, *Seminar: die Hermeneutik und die Wissenschaften* (Frankfurt: Suhrkamp, 1978). – Ricoeur's note.

(a) At a *first* still *formal level*, they all agree in distinguishing between the universal aim of hermeneutics and the limited character of the *fields* of experience from which reflection starts. On this basis, one can denounce the limited character of the problematic of the human sciences, but, even in *Wahrheit und Methode*, this problematic does not cover the whole space reflected upon; historical experience is framed between the experience of art and of language. The experience of art even has a quite special priority, inasmuch as it makes the anteriority of the truth of the thing over aesthetic judgment clearly appear. As for the experience of language, it certainly has its own limit, if we reduce the problematic of the text to that of translation, but it does contain the principle for surpassing all the limited domains taken as starting points.

This is why we can suggest other starting points than those adopted by *Wahrheit und Methode*. For example, ancient rhetoric was to Greek philosophy what hermeneutics has been for Lutheranism, then for German Romanticism, namely, the enterprise of facing up to the dissolution of a solid tie to tradition, an effort to take hold of something vanishing in order to bring it to intellectual awareness. Rhetoric, too, has its limits, first of all that it deals mostly with oral discourse and its influence on an audience, whereas hermeneutics deals more with the written expression of discourse. What is more, its claim to truth is limited to the order of probable arguments, ones capable of persuading someone. Yet this double limitation does not prevent us from rediscovering the universality of hermeneutics by starting from the limited problem of rhetoric. It has an unlimited ubiquity we can still verify today. Science itself, for example, is culturally efficacious only through the help of a rhetoric that calls on the resources of ordinary language. Hermeneutics appeals to the same resources when it is addressed to the *atopon* of our orientation in regard to the world and when it proposes a successful reappropriation of tradition.

Two or three examples will confirm that the universality of hermeneutics can be shown starting from other points than those explored by the heirs of the problematic of the *Geisteswissenschaften*.

Hans Robert Jauss, for example, undertakes to renew the problem of aesthetic experience within the framework of a *literary hermeneutic.*[22] The hermeneutic character of his enterprise is attested to by the care taken to grasp the relationship between author, text, and reader as a whole, without limiting oneself to an aesthetic theory of production of such works. It adds to the poetic dimension of "production" the properly aesthetic dimension of "reception" and the cathartic dimension of "communication." In this way, it links up with the rhetoric of Gorgias and Aristotle and with Kant's *Critique of Judgment*, which constitute the different sources for what one can call an aesthetic of reception. This undertaking is tied to hermeneutics in another way through its effort to reroot the reflexive moment of scholarly interpretation in the primary experience of "understanding with enjoyment."[23] In doing so, it draws directly on Gadamer's concepts of historical efficacity and application. Nevertheless, it distinguishes itself from Gadamer on two points: the "superiority of the origin" and the kind of immutability that Gadamer recognizes in classic works appears to Jauss as having to be subordinated to the productivity of understanding. But, above all, the critique that Gadamer addresses to the abstraction of aesthetic consciousness in the name of the ontological density of the work and its message about the truth leads him to misunderstand the key

[22] Hans Robert Jauss, *Kleine Apologie der ästhetischen Erfahrung* (Konstanz: Universitätsverlag, 1972); *Aesthetic Experience and Literary Hermeneutics*, trans. Michael Shaw (Minneapolis: University of Minnesota Press, 1982). See also Wolfgang Iser, *The Implicit Reader: Patterns of Communication in Prose Literature from Bunyan to Beckett* (Baltimore: Johns Hopkins University Press, 1974); *The Act of Reading: A Theory of Aesthetic Response* (Baltimore: Johns Hopkins University Press, 1978); Karl Heinz Stierle, *Text als Handlung: Perspektiven einer systematischen Literaturwissenschaft* (Munich: Fink, 1975); Jurij M. Lotman, *The Structure of the Artistic Text*, Michigan Slavic Contributions, no. 7, trans. Ronald Vroon and Gail Vroon (Ann Arbor: Department of Slavic Languages and Literature, 1977); J. Mukarovsky, *Kapitel als der Poetik* (Frankfurt: Suhrkamp, 1970); R. Kossellek and W.-D. Stempel, *Poetik und Hermeneutik: Arbeitsergebnisse einer Forschungsgruppe*, 8 vols (Munich: Fink, 1970-7); E. Coseriu, "Thesen über Sprache und Dichtung," in W. D. Stempel, ed., *Beiträge zur Textlinguistik* (Munich: Fink, 1971); Hans Blumenberg, *Der Prozess der Theoretischen Neugierde* (Frankfurt: Suhkamp, 1973). – Ricoeur's note.
[23] See Jauss, *Aesthetic Experience and Literary Hermeneutics*, 4.

concept of *aesthetic enjoyment*, which cannot really be understood starting from the outdated forms of nineteenth-century aesthetics and even less so from its exploitation by contemporary consumer culture.

This plea for "comprehensive enjoyment" opposes Jauss's literary hermeneutics to Adorno's aesthetics no less than it distinguishes it from Gadamer's.[24] For Adorno, aesthetic pleasure has been entirely corrupted by bourgeois culture, which turns it, in the form of passive consumption, into the deceptive complement of the asceticism of production. Only an aesthetic asceticism that appeals to reflection, not to enjoyment, according to Adorno, is capable of replying to the anti-*Aufklärung* of industrial culture. Jauss sets the subversive and educative function of the work of art over against this "aesthetics of negativity," in virtue precisely of the "uncontrollable" social character of aesthetic pleasure.

But aesthetic pleasure can be restored to the rank of an originary experience only if it is brought back to its sources by means of a veritable historical hermeneutic of disinterested affects. This conceptual history of pleasure, which appeals to Augustine as much as to Gorgias and Aristotle, is essentially a history of the *cathartic* function of art through rhetoric, poetics, and apologetics. It brings out the overlooked richness of aesthetic experience, which unites disclaiming the world and its transposition into an aesthetic object, the setting at a distance of social roles and ludic identification with an imaginary hero, the power of disobedience and the capacity of inaugurating new norms for action.

Jauss's work today appears well suited to fill an important lacuna in hermeneutics, namely, the study of disinterested affects in relation to fiction and poetry. The notion of aesthetic enjoyment adds in this way a new, not strictly linguistic dimension to our pre-understanding of the world in which all knowledge is rooted. This enterprise has to do with the epistemological argument in the sense that the concept of aesthetic experience reinforces the thesis of the primacy of a *sensus communis* over

[24] Theodor W. Adorno, *Aesthetic Theory*, ed. Gretel Adorno and Rolf Tiedemann; trans. Robert Hullot-Kentor (Minneapolis: University of Minnesota Press, 1997). – Ricoeur's note.

conceptual knowledge and of aesthetic communication over any theoretical consensus.

Hermeneutical reflection can also come up in other regions of human experience, as soon as we restore the concrete tissue of relations that objectification and scientific specialization tends to tear apart. Such is the case for the relations between *politics* and *ethics* in the work of Joachim Ritter, *Metaphysik und Politik: Studien zu Aristotle und Hegel*.[25] Ritter seeks first to recover the original fullness of the Greek concept of *ethos*, in its proximity to the act of inhabiting, and inhabiting a home, beyond any reduction to rules. The Aristotelian concept of *nomos* and the Hegelian one of *Sittlichkeit* find their root here. Similarly, the concrete concept *polis* needs to be restored, beyond its reduction to the State, in order to give back to it its political scope, without limiting it to the exercise of power. The Greek *Politie*, in effect, covers all the lived relations in the city – just as Hegel subordinates right, in the Kantian sense, to the overall set of ethical *institutions*. In this way, the concept of *praxis* regains its full breadth as the life governed by a community's customs.

Thus Aristotle offers the model for a way of thinking that has broken with a mythical legitimation in terms of origins and age and introduces the concrete concept of "justness" into the development of institutions toward their maturity. Hegel's philosophy of right, from its side, says the same thing: for in it, too, human beings find their reality and freedom in the concrete life lived within "ethical" institutions.

This demonstration marks the contribution of the hermeneutic history of the concepts of ethics and politics to the different attempts by hermeneutic philosophy to give force to *phronesis*

---

[25] Joachim Ritter, *Metaphysik und Politik: Studien zu Aristoteles und Hegel* (Frankfurt: Suhrkamp, 1969, 1972). An extract, " 'Politik' und 'Ethik' in der praktische Philosophie des Aristoteles," appears in Pöggeler, ed., *Hermeneutische Philosophie*, 153–76. See also Pöggeler, "Die ethisch-politische Dimension der hermeneutischen Philosophie," in Gerd G. Grau, ed., *Probleme der Ethik* (Freiburg: Alber, 1972), 45–81; and *Philosophie und Politik bei Heidegger* (Freiburg: Alber, 1972). – Ricoeur's note.

and to *sensus communis* in the face of the exclusive claims made for scientific knowledge.[26]

(b) At a *second level*, philosophical hermeneutics has directly replied to the objection that hermeneutics is limited by too narrow a concept of misunderstanding which encases it in a linguistic idealism. In doing so, it seeks to enlarge itself by integrating an explanatory or quasi-explanatory segment like that deployed by the critical social sciences into the process of understanding and interpretation.

This argument has two sides, one polemical and the other constructive.

From a merely polemical point of view, hermeneutics can point to the acknowledgment by its critics of the incomplete objective explanation of the systematic forms of distortion, as found in psychoanalysis or the critique of ideologies. As Habermas and Apel admit, explanation has to result in a new, highly mediated understanding that stems from an enlarged and improved hermeneutics. The critical social sciences can therefore have the ambition to raise understanding to a scientific level by transforming alienating distance into a controlled alienation (*kontrollierte Verfremdung*). But this critical use of objectification can be kept from falling back into a dogmatic form only if critique stops conceiving

---

[26] Re the implications of hermeneutics within the domain of biblical exegesis and Christian theology, see Michel van Esbroeck, *Herméneutique, structuralisme et exégèse: essai de logique herméneutique* (Paris: Desclée, 1968); Theodor Lorenzmeir, *Exegese und Hermeneutik: Eine vergleichende Darstellung der Theologie Rudolf Bultmanns, Herbert Brauns und Gerhard Ebelings* (Hamburg: Furche, 1968); Oswald Loretz and Walter Strolz, eds, *Die hermeneutische Frage in der Theologie* (Freiburg: Herder, 1968); Günter Strachel, *Die neue Hermeneutik: Ein Überblick* (Munich: Kösel, 1968); Pierre Fruchon, *Existence humaine et Révélation: Essais d'herméneutique* (Paris: Cerf, 1976); Eugen Biser, *Theologische Sprachtheorie und Hermeneutik* (Munich: Kösel, 1970); Gerhard Ebeling, *Word and Faith*, trans. James W. Leitch (Philadelphia: Fortress Press, 1963); Thomas M. Seebohm, *Zur Kritik der hermeneutischen Vernuft* (Bonn: Bouvier, 1972); Luigi Pareyson, *Verità e interpretazionei* (Milan: Mursia, 1971); Michael Theunissen, *Hegels Lehre vom absoluten Geist als theologsich-politischer Traktat* (Berlin: De Gruyter, 1970). – Ricoeur's note.

of itself as simply antithetical to every kind of traditional relationship to the past. To hold that reflection only works when it unmasks false claims and destroys the dogmatism of everyday *praxis* is to return to the naive opposition between reason and prejudice coming from the *Aufklärung*. This over-evaluation of reflection, always in quest of substantive relations in need of dissolution, free of all traditionality, is more deserving of the accusation of idealism than is the affirmation of universal mediation through linguistic understanding.

In this regard, the case of psychoanalysis stands out as singular. For one thing, hermeneutics has to ratify the interpretation that Apel and Habermas give of Freudian metapsychology, namely, that it constitutes only a quasi-explanation of the phenomena in question, that these have to be described as cases of systematic de-symbolization, and that re-symbolization is the goal of the whole process. But, even interpreted in this way, the psychoanalytic model deserves criticism for two reasons. For one thing, one risks placing the whole weight of the enterprise of dissolving false understandings resulting from a pseudo-understanding on such critical reflection. The psychoanalytic model then tends to reinforce the privilege of reflection in an idealist sense. For another, the model confers on physicians an exorbitant role of being experts removed from all control of social communication. At this stage, the interference in communicative dysfunctions through psychoanalytic competence becomes a perturbing factor in the social exchange. Faced with these two threats, it is important, in the first place, to recall that "hermeneutic's claim is, and remains the same. It claims to integrate into the unity of the linguistic world interpretation of that which is not understood, or that which is uncommon: 'understandable' only to the initiates" and that "the division of reflection from *praxis* contains a dogmatic error, an error that applies equally to the concept of 'emancipatory reflection.'"[27] Second, it is necessary to recall that the genuine hermeneutic situation stems from a relation between social partners irreducible to the relationship between physician and patient. What is important, therefore, is not to mix together the two language games of hermeneutic and psychoanalytic reflection. What is more, the tendency to conceive every failure of dialogue in terms of neuroses risks substituting a

[27] Gadamer, "Reply to My Critics," 278 and 289. – Ricoeur's note.

social psychiatry, which runs counter to the very project of emancipation, for the legitimate struggle between opinions, where the
adversary turns into a sick person in need of a cure, and therefore
someone needing to be submitted to medical control. Against this,
we need to recall that the relation between the sick person and the
physician is a healthy one only if the sick person voluntarily
submits to medical treatment owing to a disease that he admits to
having and in view of his seeking help to deal with it.

But, in my view, hermeneutics will preserve its credibility only
if it does not limit itself to this polemic, but goes beyond the
quasi-incantatory reaffirmation of its universality. It will attest to
its validity in regions where meaning is not brought about intentionally only if it can concretely show how explanation gets
intercalated between an initial form of behavior, close to what
occurs in ordinary conversations, and a highly mediated kind of
understanding that comes at the end. I have already shown above,
by means of a less antithetic reading of Gadamer's work, that
each one of the main categories of historical hermeneutics – traditionality, historical efficacity, fusion of horizons – appeals to a
complementary critical moment: application, historical distance,
the dialectic of question and answer. What remains to be demon-
strated is the heuristic value of this dialectical relation in precise
domains where the articulation between understanding and
explanation can be thematized and made explicit.

I have tried to broaden the breech opened by this reading of
Gadamer and to introduce a close dialectical tie between that
"belonging-to" that incorporates the interpreter into his domain
of investigation and the "distanciation" that makes possible
explanatory procedures and in general a critical attitude toward
any transmitted contents.[28] To this end, it will be helpful to place

---

[28] See my "What is a Text?" in *From Text to Action*, 105–24; *Freud and
Philosophy*; *The Conflict of Interpretations*; *The Rule of Metaphor*.
These texts should be compared to those of French authors who do not
draw on the hermeneutic tradition: Emmanuel Levinas, *Totality and
Infinity: An Essay on Exteriority*, trans. Alphonso Lingis (Pittsburgh:
Duquesne University Press, 1969); *Otherwise than Being or Beyond
Essence*, trans. Alphonso Lingis (Dordrecht: Kluwer, 1991); Henri
Maldiney, *Aîtres de la langue et demeures de la pensée* (Lausanne: L'Âge
d'homme, 1975); Michel Henry, *The Essence of Manifestation*, trans.
Girard Etzkorn (The Hague: Martinus Nijhoff, 1973); *Marx*, 2 vols
(Paris: Gallimard, 1976); partial English translation: *Marx: A Philosophy*

in parallel the epistemological situation that prevails in spheres of investigation as diverse as textual analysis, historical knowledge, and the theory of action.

The correlation between these three polemics is quite striking.

Textual analysis, taken in isolation, brings hermeneutics back to its original turf, exegesis and philology. In this sense, it indicates a limitation to the hermeneutical project of "being for the text," to speak like Gadamer. Yet, as we have seen, hermeneutics always grounds its claim to universality on the basis of a privileged experience. Textual experience is one of these, as a result of the predominant influence exercised, in France at least, by structuralism. This created a new situation, which led to a complete reevaluation of the relations between explanation and understanding. What appeared were new concepts of objectification and explanation, which owed nothing to a transfer from the natural sciences to the human sciences, as in the time of Dilthey. These new concepts were tied to the semiological model that was extended successively from phonology to lexical semantics, then to more complex linguistic entities such as the sentence, then to literary texts, myths, folklore, narratives. This semiological model brings into play the logical resources of a concept of *structure* in which a set of signs can be segmented into a finite number of basic entities, defined solely through their values of standing in opposition to one another, and capable of engendering, through a rule-governed play of combinations, every variety of linguistic manifestation. As regards textual analysis properly speaking, the application of the semiological model tends to place the text on the level of an autonomous entity, governed by codes functioning at a level comparable to that of a deep grammar and expressing themselves on the text's surface as different meaning effects. In this way, the notion of an intended meaning, conceived of as a signification meant by the author and conjectured by the reader, finds itself excluded from the field of analysis. Rejoining in this way a kind of Nietzschean critique, and basing itself on what is itself a structuralist interpretation of Marx, such as that of Althusser, structuralism then could appear to the wider public as making a major contribution to the "death of the subject,"

of Human Reality, trans. Kathleen McLaughlin (Bloomington: Indiana University Press, 1983). See also Charles Taylor, *The Explanation of Behavior* (London: Routledge and Kegan Paul, 1964). – Ricoeur's note.

diagnosed for example in Michel Foucault's *The Archaeology of Knowledge*.[29]

Faced with this semiological challenge, hermeneutics cannot confine itself to affirming that the text in itself is an abstraction imposed on the concrete and complete operation that encompasses author, text, and reader. It has to show what makes possible this abstraction of the text and what legitimates the recourse to explanation of a semiological kind. These procedures of abstraction and objectification, it seems to me, result from the very status of writing – or of inscription in general – in relation to what is spoken aloud. Writing, in effect, does amount simply to the material fixation of discourse. It is the condition of a much more fundamental phenomenon, that of the *autonomy* of the text. This is a threefold autonomy: with regard to the author's intention, with regard to the cultural situation and all the sociological conditions that applied to the production of the text, and with regard to the original audience. This signifies that the text no longer coincides with what the author meant to say; the verbal and the mental significations have different fates. This first mode of autonomy already implies the possibility that the "issue of the text" escapes the limited intended horizon of its author and that the world of the text bursts open the world of its author. But what is true about these psychological conditions is also true about the sociological ones, even if those who are ready to get rid of the author are less ready to do so when it comes to the sociological order. The work of art, the literary work, the work in general transcends its psycho-sociological conditions of production, opening itself to a unlimited series of readings, themselves situated in always different sociocultural contexts. In short, that the work de-contextualizes itself, as much from the sociological as the psychological point of view, and allows itself to be recontextualized in other ways is what happens through the act of reading. The result is that the mediation of the text cannot be treated as an extension of the dialogical situation. In dialogue, the vis-à-vis of discourse is given in advance through the colloquy itself. With writing, the original audience is transcended. Beyond it, the work itself creates its audience, virtually anyone who

[29] Michel Foucault, *The Archaeology of Knowledge*, trans. Alan Sheridan (New York: Pantheon, 1972).

knows how to read. We can see in this emancipation the most basic condition for the recognition of a critical instance at the heart of interpretation. In this sense, distanciation belongs to such mediation. We must not say therefore that the passage through explanation is destructive of intersubjective understanding. It is a mediation required by discourse itself, as soon as it is externalized by exterior marks, inscribed in "literary codes."

However the theory of the text is not the only framework in which the dialectic of explanation and understanding can be thematized. For a philosophical anthropology, the theory of the text is just one of the "places" that can contribute to the current discussion.

The *theory of history* is the second such place. Here too the opposition between positivism and anti-positivism today demands a more dialectical approach to the relations between understanding and explanation. The arguments offered by Dray, Danto, Mink, and others against the Hempelian model link up with those of Dilthey's hermeneutics. I have already referred to the taking up of this quarrel among English-speaking philosophers by continental hermeneutic philosophy. However the discussion leaves intact the problem of knowing how historical "inquiry" – as objective and explanatory – finds articulation through the understanding without which historians would be incapable of attaching the least significance to the facts they describe and explain. No doubt, it is in narrative activity itself that we have to look for this articulation of explanation on the basis of understanding.

I will dwell longer on the third "place," that of *the theory of action*. Here hermeneutics encounters, in an unexpected way, a current of analytic philosophy stemming from Wittgenstein and Austin. The parallelism between the two situations is particularly instructive in this regard. A dichotomy, similar to the one I am fighting against on the textual level, has opposed an intentionalist against a causalist camp. For the former, the language game made up of meaningful expressions such as action, intention, motive, agent, and so on is irreducible to the language game containing expressions like movement, cause, and behavior. This dualism is perhaps just as untenable as that between textual understanding and explanation. This is so for several reasons. First of all, the experience of action gets distributed along a whole gamut of cases, running from rational motivation to motivation in terms of drives where motives are causes in the Aristotelian sense of the term. Next, we ought perhaps to say that no motive has an explanatory value unless it is also a cause. In this respect, a phenomenology of the lifeworld, unfamiliar to analytic philosophy, would no doubt be the one thing, at this stage, to make clear in what way the lived body constitutes, on the ontological level, the common ground for the realms of causality and motivations, and hence also for explanation and understanding. A still more decisive argument against semantic and epistemological dualism is provided by the conditions under which action is inserted into the world. In *Explanation and Understanding*, G. H. von Wright proposes a reformulation of the conditions for an explanation, on the one hand, and for understanding, on the other, which allow bringing them together through the notion of an *intentional intervention* in the world.[30] This reformulation of the conditions for explanation stems from systems theory and a rigorous analysis of the difference between a necessary and a sufficient condition. The possibility of action is introduced by the consideration of the conditions that allow for isolating a closed system submitted to the preceding analysis. We learn to isolate a system by putting it in movement. We do this by making an action that we can do – a "basic action" in Danto's sense[31] – correspond to the initial state of a system. In this way, an agent intervenes in the course of the world. This intervention is where the understanding of our ability to act and the explanation of real systems intersect. The dichotomy between mentalism and physicalism thus seems to result from a misunderstanding of human action in the world. The result of this model of intervention is that the human sciences require a specific epistemological status that brings into play a quasi-teleological and a quasi-causal explanation. This justifies the complex status of explanation in the social sciences and in particular in history. One cannot fail to be struck by the convergence of these conclusions with those of Karl-Otto Apel concerning the status of quasi-explanations in the critique of ideologies. In the same way, von Wright, from his side, in the first chapter of

---

[30] G. H. von Wright, *Explanation and Understanding* (Ithaca: Cornell University Press, 1971). – Ricoeur's note.
[31] Arthur Danto, "What Can We Do," *Journal of Philosophy* 60 (1963): 435–45.

his book recognizes the permanence of "two traditions" of scientific investigation, which he associates with Galileo and Aristotle. So it is not surprising that his own attempt to determine the places for an epistemological intersection between these two traditions rejoins those of one part of post-Heideggerian hermeneutics.

It follows from this threefold analysis that understanding and explanation are not opposed to each other as two methods. Strictly speaking, only explanation is methodical. Understanding is the non-methodical moment that precedes, accompanies, and closes explanation. In this sense, understanding envelops explanation. In return, explanation analytically develops understanding. This is the projection on the epistemological plane of a deeper-lying implication, on the ontological plane, between the belonging of our being to beings and to being, and the distanciation that makes possible all objectification, explanation, and critique.

(c) This last comment brings us to a *third level*. It has to do with the transcendental character of hermeneutic's reflection on its own discourse.

If hermeneutics is not an anti-epistemology, but a reflection on the non-epistemological conditions of (first-level) epistemology, if it even implies an explanatory phase, a critical moment, which confers an epistemological status on (second-level) understanding, must it not assume for itself the kind of scientificity which, ever since German Idealism, gets attached to transcendental arguments? This is what R. Bubner, among others, invites us to think in an article titled "Über die wissenschaftstheoretische Rolle der Hermeneutik." Hermeneutics, in effect, is a reflection on the "presuppositions" of any understanding of the world, hence on the conditions of possibility for any knowledge built upon this understanding. In this sense, it is a transcendentalism, but one of a special type, as Apel showed in opposing a corporeal and a social a priori to an a priori of consciousness.

But this comparison goes completely astray if we lose sight of the profound difference between the claim inherent to transcendentalism to confer transparency to itself on some epistemological subject along with the system of conditions of possibility for every form of knowledge (including self-knowledge) – and the vow, so essential to hermeneutics, of a radical non-mastery and non-self-transparency of the conditions of all discourse. The historicity of these conditions consists precisely in the impossibility of a total reflection.

It is in this sense that Gadamer can say at the beginning of his *Replik*: if hermeneutics is agreement [*Verständigung*], "it seems to be especially difficult to reach agreement about the problem of hermeneutics, at least so long as unclarified concepts of science, critique, and reflection dominate the discussion."[32] The ultimate thesis of a philosophical hermeneutics is that this elucidation is unattainable. Hermeneutics is, to be sure, more than an art, it is a *Kunstlehre*. As such, it is akin to *phronesis*, which surpasses every *techne*. Therefore it encompasses a kind of reflexive knowledge. But reflection cannot become all that there is to this theoretical activity. It is always only a critical segment of a total operation that never cuts its ties to a pre-scientific understanding of the world carried by a speech community (a *Gesprächgemeinschaft*).[33] The ultimate claim to universality of hermeneutics is attached to this understanding, inasmuch as no limit can be assigned to the communicability of understanding.

This impossibility of total reflection no doubt explains why hermeneutic philosophy is more aware of its history than any other form of philosophy. In fact, it is striking how few of the discussions of hermeneutic philosophy omit beginning with a history of the hermeneutic question.[34] One can certainly see in

[32] Gadamer, "Reply to My Critics," 273. – Ricoeur's note.
[33] Ibid., 277. – Ricoeur's note.
[34] Norbert Heinrichs, *Bibliographie der Hermeneutik und ihrer Anwendungsbereiche seit Schleiermacher* (Düsseldorf: Philosophia, 1968). Dilthey's well-known work – the *Preisschrift* of 1860 – *Leben Schleiermachers*, published only in 1966 as edited by Martin Redker in the *Gesammelte Schriften*, vol. 14:2 (Göttigen: Vandenhoeck and Ruprecht), was already a history of hermeneutics. [An edition had in fact already been published in 1870 (Berlin: G. Reimer). – eds] The same may be said of Dilthey's shorter text from 1900: *Die Entstehung der Hermeneutik* in *Gesammelte Schriften*, vol. 5, 317–38; "The Rise of Hermeneutics," trans. Fredric R. Jameson and Rudolf A. Makkreel, in Dilthey, *Hermeneutics and the Study of History, Selected* Works, vol. 4, ed. Rudolf A. Makkreel and Frithjof Rodi (Princeton: Princeton University Press, 1996), 235–58. Hans-Georg Gadamer, "Hermeneutik," in J. Ritter, ed., *Historisches Wörterbuch der Philosophie* (Basel: Schwabe, 1974); Gadamer, "Hermeneutik," in Raymond Klibansky, ed., *Contemporary Philosophy: A Survey* (Firenze: La Nuova Italia, 1969), 360–72;

that history an objective sense, an "evident" teleology. This is of an increasing radicalization and universalization, proceeding from an initial stage where hermeneutics comes down to a collection of practical rules scattered among the three domains of biblical exegesis, classical philology, and jurisprudence to a second stage where hermeneutics rises to an epistemological reflection on understanding in general, then finally to a third stage where hermeneutics thinks of itself as hermeneutic philosophy and where epistemology gets rooted in ontology. But the teleology of this history of hermeneutics – which does not differ from that manifested by other schools of thought in their development – does not constitute the profound historicity of hermeneutics; namely, the fact that it itself belongs to a history of thought that is not entirely transparent to itself. This is why this history does not reduce to the autobiography of a movement, but instead constitutes a hermeneutic interpretation of its own history. This does not mean that we cannot say that hermeneutics was born when tradition had lost its normative force, beginning in the era of the humanists and Luther, then in the age of the *Aufklärung* and of Romanticism, and that its Heideggerian and post-Heideggerian formulation was contemporary, with a more radical crisis having to do with the transmission of culture; one having to do with the clash between the cultural prestige of science and the suspicion infecting the heart of modern culture inaugurated by Marx, Nietzsche, and Freud.

A second feature of finitude, having to do with its discourse, and hence inherent in its own *Verstehen*, needs to be added to this first feature of finitude characteristic of the "situation" of hermeneutics, namely, that hermeneutic philosophy cannot escape the history of metaphysics. When it insists on the transcendental character of its reflection, it inscribes itself among the

Pöggler, "Einführung," *Hermeneutischen Philosophie*, 7–71. A selection of extracts from authors belonging to the "prehistory" of hermeneutics, "Romantic" hermeneutics, and "Dilthey and his School," and some contemporary thinkers, including Lipps, can be found in Pöggler and Boehm, eds, *Seminar: Philosophische Hermeneutik*. See also Richard Palmer, *Hermeneutics: Interpretation Theory in Schleiermacher, Dilthey, Heidegger, and Gadamer* (Evanston: Northwestern University Press, 1969); Eugenio Coseriu, *Die Geschichte der Sprachphilosophie von der Antik bis zur Gegenwart: Eine Übersicht*, 2 vols (Stuttgart: TBL-Verlag, 1969–72). – Ricoeur's note.

philosophies of the subject. When it deals with the differences between the human sciences and those of nature, it situates itself within the heritage of the Hegelian philosophy of the objective Spirit. When it attempts to connect the productions of this spirit back to expressions of life, it engages in a perhaps impossible synthesis between a philosophy of spirit and one of life. When it relates our historical understanding of the world to Dasein, it perhaps remains the prisoner of a philosophical anthropology that sums up and resumes without really abolishing the triple heritage of Kant, Hegel, and Romanticism. Heidegger's *Kehre* makes no sense if we do not admit this. As for Heidegger's philosophy subsequent to this *Kehre* and his successive attempts to rethink ontology, then to transcend it to the benefit of a thinking both closer to and distant from poeticizing, this attests that we are never done with the speculative tradition of Western philosophy, and that its "destruction" can only be a kind of more originary thinking of this tradition and what it has thought.

This is the underlying reason for discussion within hermeneutics over its own history. This discussion is not a chronological preface to an atemporal task. It is a struggle, within its consciousness of finitude, to make explicit its implicit presuppositions, its unsaid, and it knows, in this regard, that an exhaustive explication is impossible. This finitude of interpretation, which affects the discourse of hermeneutics about itself, is what finally prevents this discourse from assimilating itself to a transcendental philosophy.

The Confrontation between Hermeneutics and Analytic Philosophy

I assigned myself two tasks in undertaking this report: to reflect on the conditions and presuppositions of the discourse of hermeneutics, and to situate this discourse in relation to those philosophies for which logical and epistemological preoccupations take pride of place. We have finished the first task. As for the second one, it has largely been anticipated in our discussion of the limits of hermeneutics. In particular, when we referred to the presumed analogy between the hermeneutics of language, in the sense of Heidegger and Gadamer, and "language games" in the sense of the later Wittgenstein. The time has come to take up this discussion for itself, inasmuch as it has become one of the more important topics in the post-Heideggerian period.

That the two currents of thought meet on the question of language is a truism today. But this encounter is not sufficient to create a convergence. A divergence rather than a convergence seems instead to take place, even if, subsequently, deepening this divergence suggests more subtle forms of interaction.

Karl-Otto Apel, who opened this discussion, proposes taking as a starting point the superficial analogy between the function both sides assign to language in understanding the world.[35] Starting from there, he institutes two levels of confrontation. At the level of Carnap and the Wittgenstein of the *Tractatus*, for one; at the level of the *Logical Investigations*, for the other.

At the first level, one can sum up the oppositions in terms of an inverted relation between *meaning* and *understanding*. On the side of hermeneutics, from Luther to Schleiermacher, meaning, we can say, is not doubtful. It is understanding that is a problem. The credit given to meaning remains, even when meaning has lost its normative force. For example, with Dilthey, meaning is the expression of infinite life. Then, with Heidegger, the ground of meaning no longer lies in life but in Dasein, which has already always understood its insertion in the world. With Gadamer, the certitude of meaning again precedes from an interrogation of understanding: the beauty of the work of art has already taken hold of me before I judge it, tradition already carries me before I place it at a distance, language has already instructed me, before I master it as a system of available signs. In all these ways, belonging to meaning precedes every logic of language. Which is why hermeneutics is finally a struggle against misunderstanding of what has always already been understood; whether this misunderstanding proceeds from confusions arising out of metaphysics

---

[35] Karl-Otto Apel, "Wittgenstein and Heidegger: Language Games and Life Forms: A Critical Comparison," trans. Christopher McCann, in Apel, *From a Transcendental-Semiotic Point of View*, ed. Marianna Papstephanou (Manchester: Manchester University Press, 1998), 122–59; "Heideggers philosophische Radikalisierung der 'Hermeneutik' und die Frage das Problem des hermeneutischen Verstehens," in Loretz and Strolz, eds, *Die hermeneutische Frage in der Theologie*, 86–152; "Wittgenstein and the Problem of Hermeneutic Understanding," in *Towards a Transformation of Philosophy*, 1–45. – Ricoeur's note.

(a confusing of the being we ourselves are and subsisting and manipulable beings; a confusion of being as being with a supreme being in onto-theology; a misunderstanding of the ontological difference between being and be-ings); or the misunderstanding proceeds from methodological objectification and alienation.

For analytic philosophy, it is not understanding that is in question, but rather the presupposition of meaning. The question is one of the *criterion* that makes it possible to distinguish between what can be taken as meaningful a priori and what is meaningless. The only way to decide is to establish a priori criteria of meaning, prior to any consideration of content. Here, moreover, is where the divergences begin within analytic philosophy: some place the criterion in the logical form of language, others in the empirical verifiability of propositions, others still in one or another form of practical efficacity or some operational value. But all three forms of a "critique of meaning" lead to the conclusion that the so-called pre-understanding invoked by hermeneutical philosophy is stated in propositions that turn out, not to be false, but lacking meaning. If they seem meaningful, it is because they present, for a superficial grammar, a structure similar to that of meaningful propositions.

In this regard, the attacks on hermeneutics issuing from the partisans of the first criterion of meaning – in terms of the logical form of language – are the most important ones. They are precisely those of Carnap and the *Tractatus*. Their objection can be stated briefly in the following terms: hermeneutics cannot formulate its statements about the meaning of being except by treating being as a predicate, hence without falling into the confusion already denounced by Kant in his critique of the classical proofs for God's existence. Faced with this criticism, the only resource hermeneutics has is to riposte that the criteria of meaning being applied to it include unacknowledged presuppositions that turn out to be hermeneutic. That is, the "logical" criteria for meaning express a way of thinking that has in advance limited all being that can be encountered to subsisting or ready-to-hand things. In other words, *Sprachlogik* and *Grammatik* remain within the limits of an ontology of subsisting or ready-to-hand things. But it is one of the tasks of hermeneutics to preserve the difference between what is ready-to-hand and that in view of which things are ready-to-hand in general. And it is to preserve just this difference that hermeneutics appeals to a dimension of language that does not fall under propositional analysis and is instead the site where the prior assumption about the meaning of what is ready-to-hand and what not occurs. Projecting this dimension of language on the grammatical and logical planes does not exhaust its intention or its efficacity. This is why a discussion about the predicative use of the word "being" in no way exhausts the pre-propositional "meaning" of hermeneutic statements, following the already referred to distinction between an apophantic and a hermeneutical logic.

The confrontation at the level of the *Tractatus* therefore seems to end in a hung jury. Other authors, though, have tried to discern certain convergences between Heidegger and the *Tractatus*. Jörg Zimmermann, for example, expanding an opening of Helmut Fahrenbach's, takes the question of possibility of a homology of structure postulated by the *Tractaus* between the meaning of propositions and states of affairs of the world to be a hermeneutical one.[36] In this regard, the thesis that meaning "shows itself," without our being able to "say" what makes possible the *Darstellung* [representational] function of statements, defines the hermeneutic framework of the *Tractatus*. The thesis that "a proposition shows its meaning" constitutes Wittgenstein's most general response to the hermeneutic question about the conditions of possibility for the understanding of meaning. The same thing must be said about his affirmation that "language takes care of itself."[37] Reflection on the possible limits of "meaning," hence on the boundary between *sinnvollen* [meaningful] and *unsinnig* [nonsense] and its "solipsistic" implication, for which the subject would constitute the limit of the world, also has a hermeneutic import. Finally, the negative thesis that philosophy cannot constitute itself as a metalanguage capable of explaining its relation to language as

---

[36] Helmut Fahrenbach, "Die logisch-hermeneutische Problemstellung in Wittgensteins 'Tractatus'," in *Hermeneutik und Dialektik*, 2: 25–54; "Positionen und Probleme gegenwärtigen Philosophie, Teil II: Philosophie der Sprache," *Theologische Rundschau* 35 (1970): 277–306; 36 (1971): 125–44, 221–43; Jörg Zimmermann, *Wittgensteins sprachphilosophische Hermeneutik* (Frankfurt: Klostermann, 1975). – Ricoeur's note.

[37] Zimmermann, *Wittgensteins sprachphilosophische Hermeneutik*, 7, 23–4, 50. – Ricoeur's note.

an object, as well as the positive thesis that is its counterpart, that the reflective relation of philosophy to language is not expressed in *sinnvollen* propositions, but rather in *Erläuterungen* [clarifications], which are *unsinnig* because they show rather than state things, is hermeneutic. To which we can add that the fact that Wittgenstein's reflections on saying, showing, and remaining silent added their influence to similar points made by Hofmannsthal, Rilke, and Kafka constitutes an indirect testimony to the implicitly hermeneutic character of the theses of the *Tractatus*.

These points raised by Zimmermann do not formally contradict those of Karl-Otto Apel. If there is a Wittgensteinian hermeneutic, it is precisely another hermeneutic. The question that this poses will be precisely to know whether one can speak of hermeneutics outside the "hermeneutic" tradition.

The more apparent relationship between Heidegger's hermeneutics and Wittgenstein's *Philosophical Investigations* allows us to approach this problem.

It is, in fact, at this level that Karl-Otto Apel sees the closest analogy and the profoundest divergence between these two thinkers. The analogy cannot be doubted: does not the link Wittgenstein establishes between language games and forms of life call to mind the tie Heidegger detected between understanding and care? Does not Wittgenstein's idea that all knowledge about the world is articulated on a linguistic level find an echo in Gadamer's notion of a linguistic dimension of the world? Is not the critique of a private language in the *Philosophical Investigations* prolonged in the idea of a prior agreement, of a cultural transmission, common to Gadamer and his successors, including Habermas and Apel? And does not the theory of speech-acts link up with the anticipations of a *hermeneutical logic* to be found in Hans Lipps? This attempted rapprochement seems further encouraged by the fact that both schools have a common adversary, classical metaphysics, whether this is expressed as the thing in itself, the absolute subject, or solipsism. For the one, these are pseudo-problems unmasked by their depth grammar, for the other they are the most deeply rooted forms of misunderstanding to be found in Western "metaphysics." Yet a gap opens precisely between a critique that dissolves the problem as a metaphorical illusion and thought that sees dogmatic forms in the speculative tradition of the West which it is possible to return to a more primal form. The consequence of this profound difference in how the past is understood is a very different evaluation of the very task of philosophy. If there may be a difficulty in defining hermeneutics as a kind of transcendental reflection, this definition is not problematic but rather simply impossible starting from the *Philosophical Investigations*. In the eyes of hermeneutic philosophy, the theory of language games is incapable of reflecting on its own conditions of possibility. If discourse is always caught up in a language game, how is reflection on this linguistic condition possible? If the understanding of being gets identified with a language game, in what language can we talk about it? If we do not want to reduce philosophical activity to a verbal convention, we need to be able to root the philosophical language game in an understanding of being in the world prior to every language game. Here is where the divergent evaluations of the philosophical tradition develops its real consequences: if all speculative language serves as a vehicle for pseudo-problems that it is necessary, not to resolve, but to dissolve, does not this also apply to the same philosophy that says this? Karl-Otto Apel does not exclude that a new convergence might be born from this final divergence. But it is still too early to say. The most one can do is to make the following twofold suggestion: every attempt by analytic philosophy to escape pure conventionalism, or to account for a fundamental reflection by language on its own determinations and institutions, points in the direction of a hermeneutic of language. Conversely, every effort of philosophical hermeneutics to define the conditions for a propositional inscription of its *hermeneutical logic* seems to lead toward a reflection on the relation, as much creative as critical, between the language game of philosophy and the other institutionalized language games. What is at stake in this debate is the relation of philosophy to its own history. Does the philosophy of language mark an unprecedented break with that tradition, that is, a break that no longer understands what it breaks with? Or is the "destruction of metaphysics" the path leading to a mediated reappropriation of the tradition of speculative philosophy, that might permit the historical dialogue of humanity with itself to continue? Karl-Otto Apel's twofold confrontation between *Sinnkritik* and *Sprachhermeneutik* ends with this question.

Zimmermann focuses on another issue: to him, the hermeneutics of language games seems all the more fruitful in that it owes nothing to the Romantic tradition, nor to the philosophical enterprise of Heidegger, Lipps, and Gadamer, but proceeds exclusively from a critical reflection on its own prejudices, which link up with those of rationalist-empiricist thought. At this price this hermeneutic brings a complement and a corrective to hermeneutics. The hermeneutic character of Wittgenstein's reflection resides essentially in the designation of natural language as the basis and horizon of every understanding of meaning. One can, in this way, speak of a hermeneutic circle in Wittgenstein. It was present, starting with the *Tractatus*, in the thesis of an isomorphism between a proposition and a state of affairs, as well as in its corollary, the impossibility of doing philosophy of language from the outside. However, with the *Philosophical Investigations*, the articulation of the pre-understanding included in language no longer consists in the "letting it be seen" of an a priori structure of an ontological nature, but in the recognition of *factual* presuppositions of speaking within the context of forms of life. Zimmermann, it is true, notes that the possible rapprochement between Wittgenstein and Heidegger–Gadamer holds only insofar as one can set aside a pragmaticist, even behaviorist, interpretation of the *Investigations*. The recourse made to a "depth grammar" is no less opposed to "external" criteria of behavior than to ones "internal" to a private mind. Behaviorism, in other words, is just the inverse version of a mentalism.[38] The hermeneutics of the *Philosophical Investigations* consists instead in the contingency of the grammatical order, in that it constitutes the factual a priori that precedes any relationship to the world. Zimmermann does agree with Apel in denouncing the conflict between the claim to universality by a philosophical grammar that excludes any reflections from the outside and its critical claim to destroy *one* specific language game, that of "metaphysics."[39] But Zimmermann's important reservations concerning Wittgenstein's hermeneutic matter less than do the consequences he draws for hermeneutics itself from the very existence of a hermeneutic that gets constituted outside the sphere of reflection on the conditions of possibility of the human sciences.

[38] Ibid., 224–37. – Ricoeur's note.
[39] Ibid., 251. – Ricoeur's note.

In this regard, the important convergences referred to above may serve to outline the framework for a broader hermeneutic in which the hermeneutic of the human sciences would receive, as already stated, a complement and above all a corrective. The complement becomes clearer if we do not limit ourselves, like Karl-Otto Apel, to a comparison between *Sein und Zeit* and the *Philosophical Investigations*. The conception of the autonomy of language, from *Unterwegs zur Sprache*, casts a new light on Wittgenstein's affirmation that language "takes care of itself."[40] A still more secret kinship is uncovered if we take into account Wittgenstein's writings on ethics, aesthetics, and religion along with everything he says that can be inscribed under the heading of what shows itself, as well as what remains silent, and maybe, what speaks in a different way.[41] Yet the corrective may be more important than the complement. What is interesting about Wittgenstein's hermeneutic is that its origin does not lie in the problematic of the human sciences and does not take historical transmission as its axis. For this hermeneutic, historicity comes second, it is even suspect in principle, in relation to the facticity of everyday language games. The least effect of including Wittgenstein within the field of hermeneutics will be to challenge the privileged place given to the historicity of linguistic meditations. Yet one has to ask oneself if the divorce between a philosophy for which something continuous speaks to us in the speculative tradition of the West and a philosophy that puts the principal accent on current discourse practice in its everyday contexts is irremediable. In this, thanks to this discussion, we can see a certain ramification of the very concept of hermeneutics indicated, one where it risks losing its identity.

First of all, is it a *Kunstlehre* of linguistic understanding for which the interpretation of texts remains the privileged model? Or does language itself become secondary in relation to an

---

[40] Martin Heidegger, *On the Way to Language*, trans. Peter D. Hertz (New York: Harper and Row, 1971).
[41] Allan Janik and Stephen Toulmin, *Wittgenstein's Vienna* (New York: Simon and Schuster, 1973); Gerd Brand, *Die grundlegenden Texte von Ludwig Wittgenstein* (Frankfurt: Suhrkamp, 1975); Jacques Bouveresse, *La Parole malheureuse: de l'alchimie linguistique à la grammaire philosophique* (Paris: Minuit, 1971). – Ricoeur's note.

"experience of understanding" that may not be verbal, as in the case of aesthetic pleasure?

If we choose the first branch of this alternative, must we say that the task of understanding is to "rethink" what was once "thought," to "reproduce" what was once "produced"? Or is understanding itself "productive" of meaning in new cultural and life situations? For the first hypothesis, the basic experience remains *historical mediation*, that is, finally, the tradition that addresses us and makes us think before we are in a state where we can reflect upon it. For the second hypothesis, historical mediation comes second in relation to the new contextualization of discourse in hitherto unknown situations of everyday life.

But the first hypothesis divides in turn into two: with regard to cultural transmission, is the accent on the authority of tradition, as bearing meaning and possible truth? Or is it on the critical instance that transforms every received heritage into a "circumstance"?

Something more must be added to this alternative: is hermeneutics itself *universal*, because all understanding falls under its competence? Or is it limited, if it is true that the structures of existence, be they individual or social, are not all intentional? The first hypothesis permits innumerable *mediations* for an unending expanding and deepening of what remains an interpretation. For the second hypothesis, understanding is a limited mode that leaves explanation outside itself and calls for the mediation of a third critical or dialectical discipline. This same alternative redoubles itself: if all understanding is historically mediated, must we say that hermeneutic reflection on hermeneutics is too? Or should we say that we understand the contextual relativity of interpretation only in light of a regulative idea of "rational" discourse or of "unlimited, unhindered communication"? In the first case, hermeneutics confesses its own finitude, at the very heart of its universal claim; in other words, its "epochal" character, wherein are reflected its dependence on other "epochs" of being and thinking. In the second case, hermeneutics transcends itself in reflection and reinscribes itself in the tradition of transcendental philosophy. In the first case, the hermeneutics of hermeneutics remains faithful to its basic thesis, but excludes all scientificity. In the second case, it pleads for a concept of scientificity distinct from the concept (at least in English) of science, but it denies its thesis about the priority of pre-understanding over reflection.

4

Hermeneutics of the Idea of Revelation

The question of revelation is a formidable question. I readily admit that, until now, I have not considered it directly, but always obliquely and through detours.[1] I take it up today as a challenge that must be taken up, if one is not to deny the virtue of *Redlichkeit*, intellectual honesty, that Nietzsche denied to Christians. But why is the question so formidable? In my opinion, it is not only because it is the last or the first question for faith, but also because it has been obscured by so many false debates that the recovery of a real question in itself constitutes an enormous task.

The way of posing the question, which, more than any other, I will seek to overcome, is the one that sets in opposition an authoritarian and opaque concept of revelation and a concept of

---

[1] The material in this lecture was first presented at the "Symposium sur l'idée de la revelation" at the Faculté Universitaires Saint-Louis in Brussels, on February 17. 1976, then published in Ricoeur et al., *La Revelation* (Publications des Facultés Universitaires Saint-Louis, 1977), 15–54, along with the discussion that followed on that occasion (207–36). It was first presented in English in a somewhat condensed form as the Dudleian Lecture at the Harvard University Divinity School on November 11, 1976. This earlier translation, here slightly revised, appeared first in the *Harvard Theological Review* 70 (1977): 1–37, then in Paul Ricoeur, *Essays on Biblical Interpretation*, ed. Lewis S. Mudge (Philadelphia: Fortress Press, 1980), 73–118.

reason that claims to be its own master and transparent to itself. This is why my presentation will be a battle on two fronts: it seeks to get to a concept of revelation and a concept of reason that, without ever coinciding, can at least enter into a living dialectic and together engender something like an understanding of faith.

The Originary Expressions of Revelation

The first part of my remarks will be devoted to rectifying the concept of revelation so that we may get beyond what I have spoken of as the accepted opaque and authoritarian understanding of this concept.

By an opaque concept, I mean that amalgamation of three levels of language familiar to a certain traditional teaching about revelation: the level of the confession of faith, where the *lex credendi* is not separated from the *lex orandi*; the level of ecclesial dogma, where a historic community interprets for itself and for others the understanding of faith specific to its tradition; and finally, the body of doctrines imposed by the magisterium as the rule of orthodoxy. The particular amalgamation that I deplore and that I am seeking to combat is always made in terms of the third level, which is why it is not just opaque, but also authoritarian. For it is on this level that the ecclesiastical magisterium is exercised and this is where it puts its stamp of authority on matters of faith. In this sense, the rule that we have to believe contaminates, in descending order, the levels that I have just named in ascending order. The doctrine of a confessing community loses the meaning of the historical character of its interpretations and places itself under the tutelage of the fixed assertions of the magisterium. In turn, the confession of faith loses the suppleness and fluidity of preaching and is identified with the dogmatic assertions of a tradition and with the theological discourse of one school, whose ruling categories are imposed by the magisterium. It is from this amalgamation and this contamination that arises the massive and impenetrable concept of "revealed truth" – often expressed in the plural, "revealed truths" – in order to emphasize the discursive character of the dogmatic propositions that are taken to be identical with the founding faith.

My intention is not to deny the specificity of the work of formulating dogma, whether at the ecclesial level or the level of theological investigation. But I do affirm its derived and subordinate character. This is why I am going to endeavor to carry the notion of revelation back to its most originary level, the one, which for the sake of brevity, I have called the discourse of faith or the confession of faith.

In what manner is the category of revelation included in this discourse? This question seems all the more legitimate to me in that there is little for the philosopher to receive or learn from a level of discourse organized in terms of his own speculative categories, for he then discovers fragments borrowed from his own discourse, and the travesty of this discourse that results from its authoritarian and opaque use. On the other hand, he may receive and learn much from a non-speculative discourse – from what Whitehead called barbaric discourse, because it had not yet been illuminated by the philosophical logos. What is more, it is an old conviction of mine that the philosopher's conversation partner in this type of argument is not the theologian, but the believer who is informed by the exegete; I mean the believer who seeks to understand himself through a better understanding of the texts of his faith.

The principal benefit of such a return to the origin of theological discourse is that from the outset it places before reflection a variety of expressions of faith, all modulated by the variety of discourses within which the faith of Israel and then of the early church is inscribed. Instead of a monolithic concept of revelation, which is obtained by transforming these different forms of discourse into propositions, we encounter a pluralistic, polysemic, and at most an analogical concept of revelation – where the very term revelation, as we shall see, is borrowed from one of these forms of discourse.

Prophetic Discourse

Which of the biblical forms of discourse should be taken as the basic referent for a meditation on revelation? It seems legitimate to begin by taking prophetic discourse as our basic axis of inquiry. Indeed, it is this discourse that declares itself to be pronounced "in the name of..." And exegetes have rightly pointed out the importance of its introductory formula: "The word of Yahweh came to me, saying, 'Go and proclaim in the hearing of Jerusalem, ...'" (Jer. 2:1). We have here the original nucleus of the idea of revelation. The prophet presents himself as not speaking in his own name, but in the name of another. So here the idea of revelation appears as identified with the idea of a double author of what is said and written. Revelation is the speech of another behind the speech of the prophet. The prophetic genre's central position is so decisive that the third article of the Nicene creed devoted to the Holy Spirit declares: "We believe in the Holy Spirit... who spoke through the prophets."

Yet if we separate the prophetic mode of discourse from its context, and especially if we separate it from that narrative discourse that is so important for the constituting of Israel's faith, as well as for the faith of the early church, we risk imprisoning the idea of revelation in too narrow a concept, the concept of the speech of another. This narrowness is indicated by several features. One is that prophecy remains bound to the literary genre of the oracle, which itself is one tributary of those archaic techniques, such as divination, omens, dreams, casting dice, astrology, etc., that sought to tap the secrets of the divine. It is true that for the great prophets of Israel, symbolic visions are subordinated to the eruption of the Word, which may appear without any accompanying vision. But it also remains true that the explicit form of two voices speaking tends to link the notion of revelation to that of inspiration conceived of as one voice behind another. When extended to the other forms of biblical discourse we are going to consider, this concept of revelation, taken as a synonym for revelation, leads to the idea of scripture as dictated, as something whispered in someone's ear. The idea of revelation is then confused with the idea of a double author of sacred texts. Any access to a less subjective manner of understanding revelation is prematurely cut off, and the very idea of inspiration, as arising from meditation on the Holy Spirit, is deprived of the enrichment it might receive from those forms of discourse that are less easily interpreted in terms of a voice behind a voice or of a double author of scripture. Finally, the ancient bond between an oracle and techniques of divination establishes an almost invincible association between the idea of prophecy and that of an unveiling of the future. This association tends to impose the idea, in turn, that the content of revelation is to be assimilated to a design, in the sense of a plan that would give a goal to the unfolding of history. This concentration on the idea of revelation as "God's plan" is all the more insistent in what apocalyptic literature, which was subsequently grafted on to the prophetic trunk, calls the "Apocalypse" – i.e., revelation in the strict sense of the word – the unveiling of God's plans concerning the "last days." The idea of revelation then tends to become identified with the idea of a premonition of the end of history. The "last days" are the divine secret that apocalyptic discourse proclaims by means of dreams, visions, symbolic transpositions of earlier writings, etc. In this way, the much richer notion, as we shall see, of the divine promise tends to be reduced to the dimensions of a divination applied to the "end of time."

Narrative Discourse

For these reasons, we must not limit ourselves to simply identifying revelation and prophecy. The other modes of the discourse of faith bear this out. The one that has to be placed in the front rank is surely that narrative genre of discourse that dominates the Pentateuch, as well as the synoptic Gospels and the Book of Acts.

What does revelation mean as regards these texts? Should we say that, as with the prophetic texts, these texts have a double author, the writer and the spirit that guides him? Or should we really attend above all else to the side of the narrator? Linguists, such as Emile Benveniste, for example, and theoreticians of narrative discourse have noted that in narration the author often disappears and it is as though the events recounted themselves. Historical assertions, that is, the telling of past events, Benveniste says, in his "The Correlations of Tense in the French Verb," exclude the speaker's intervening in the story.[2] Every linguistic form of autobiography is banished. There is no longer even a narrator: "events are posited as though they were produced to

[2] Emile Benveniste, "The Correlations of Tense in the French Verb," in *Problems in General Linguistics*, trans. Mary Elizabeth Meek (Coral Gables, FL: University of Miami Press, 1971), 205–16. – Ricoeur's note.

the extent that they appeared on the horizon of history. No one speaks here; the events seem to narrate themselves."[3] Can we annul this specific feature of narration by advancing the trivial argument that someone nevertheless wrote it and that he stands in a relation to his text analogous to that of the prophet and the double author of prophecy? I am well aware that when the Nicene Creed proclaims: "who spoke through the prophets," the creed enfolds narration into prophecy, following the tradition that Moses was the unique narrator of the Pentateuch and that he was the prophet par excellence. But in following this route, has not the classical theory of inspiration missed the instruction proper to the narrative genre?

What I am here suggesting is that we should pay more attention to the things recounted than to the narrator and his prompter. We then see that it is within the story itself that Yahweh is designated in the third person as the ultimate *actant* – to use A.-J. Greimas's category – that is, he is one of the characters signified by the narration itself, and intervenes along with the other actants in the goings on.[4] It is not a double narrator, a double speaking subject, but a double actant, and consequently a double object of the story, that we need to think about.

Let us follow this trail. Where does it lead? Essentially to meditation on the character of the events recounted, such as the election of Abraham, the Exodus, the anointing of David, etc., and, for the early church, the resurrection of Christ. Is it not to the very character of these events that a sense of revelation gets attached? Which one?

What is noteworthy about these events is that they do not simply occur and then pass away. They mark an epoch and they engender a history. In this vein, the Jewish scholar Emil Fackenheim speaks of "history-making events." These events found an epoch because they have the twofold characteristic of both founding a community and of delivering it from a great danger, which, moreover, may take diverse forms. To speak here of revelation is to qualify the events in question as transcendent in relation to the

[3] Ibid., 208. – Ricoeur's note.
[4] See A.-J. Greimas, *Structural Semantics*, trans. Daniele McDowell, Ronald Schleifer, and Alan Velie (Lincoln: University of Nebraska Press, 1983).

ordinary course of history. The whole faith of Israel and of the early church is tied up here in the confession of the transcendent character of such nuclear, founding, and instituting events.

As Gerhard von Rad has established in his great work, *The Theology of the Old Testament* (and principally in volume 1, "The Theology of Traditions"), Israel confessed God essentially by ordering its sagas, traditions, and stories around a few kernel events from which meaning spread throughout the whole structure.[5] Von Rad believes he has discovered the most ancient kernel of the Hebraic Credo in a text such as Deut. 26:5b–10b, which reads:

> A wandering Aramaean was my father; he went down to Egypt and lived there as an alien, few in number, and there he became a nation, great, mighty and populous. When the Egyptians treated us harshly and afflicted us, by imposing hard labor on us, we cried to the Lord, the God of our ancestors. The Lord heard our voice and saw our affliction, our toil and our oppression. The Lord brought us out of Egypt with a mighty hand and an outstretched arm, with a terrifying display of power, and with signs and wonders; and he brought us into this place and gave us this land, a land flowing with milk and honey. So now I bring the first fruit of the ground that you, O Lord, have given me. (NSRV)

(Notice how the recitation that first designates Yahweh in the third person, as the supreme actant, then raises to an invocation that addresses God in the second person: "So now I bring the first fruit of the ground that you, O Lord, have given me." We will return to this change from the use of the third to the second person when we discuss the hymnic literature.)

Let us continue our examination of the narrative form.[6] What is essential here is the emphasis on the founding event or events

---

[5] Gerhard von Rad, *Old Testament Theology*, 2 vols, trans. D. M. G. Stalker (New York: Harper, 1962–5).

[6] In the discussion that followed the presentation of this lecture in Brussels, Ricoeur said, "I think that the first fault line that breaks with the Greek world, is the narrative element. Narrative's power is that it designates God not as an idea, a principle, an ideal, or as a spatial figure of the cosmos, but as actually historical, as acting historically" (*La Révélation*, 210).

as the imprint, mark, or trace of God. Confession takes place through their narration. The problematic of inspiration is in no way the primary consideration. The mark of God is in history before being in speech. It is only secondarily in speech, inasmuch as this history itself is brought to language, through the speech-act of narration. Here is where a "subjective" moment comparable to prophetic inspiration comes to the fore, but only after the fact. This subjective moment is no longer the narration insofar as the events recount themselves, but the event of narration insofar as it is presented by a narrator to a community. The word event is thus emphasized at the expense of the first intentionality of the narrative confession, or rather the confessing narrative. The latter does not distinguish itself from the things recounted and the events that present themselves in the story. It is therefore for a second-order reflection that the questions "*who* is speaking? *who* is telling the story?" get detached from *what* is narrated and said. It is for this reflection that the author of the narration comes to the fore and appears to be related to his writing as the prophet is to his words. This narrator, in turn, may by analogy be said to speak in the name of... , and then he is a prophet; the Spirit also speaks through him. But this absorption of narration into prophecy runs the risk of annulling the specific feature of the narrative confession: its aiming at God's trace in the event.

To recognize the specificity of this form of discourse, therefore, is to guard ourselves against a certain narrowness of any theology of the Word, which only attends to word events. In the encounter with what we could call an idealism of the word event, we must reaffirm the realism of the event of history – as is indicated today by the work of a theologian such as Wolfhart Pannenberg in his attempts to rectify the one-sided emphasis of Ernst Fuchs and Gerhard Ebeling. What is more, narration includes prophecy in a certain manner in its province, insofar as prophecy too is narrative in its fashion. Indeed, the meaning of prophecy is not exhausted by the subjectivity of the prophet. Prophecy moves forward toward the "Day of Yahweh," which the prophet says will not be a day of joy, but of terror. This phrase, the "Day of Yahweh," announces something like an event, which will be to impending history what the founding events were to the history recounted in the great biblical narratives. The tension between narration and prophecy therefore first occurs at the level of the event, in the dialectic of the event. The same history that narration founds as certain is suddenly undercut by the menace announced in the prophecy. The supporting pedestal totters. Yahweh's accompanying Israel turns into terror. It is the structure of history that is at stake here, not just the quality of the word that speaks about it. And revelation is straightaway implicated in this now narrative, now prophetic understanding of history.

Did we say understanding? But this understanding cannot be articulated within any specific form of knowledge, within any system. Between the security conferred by the recitation of the founding events and the threat announced by the prophet there is no rational synthesis, no triumphant dialectic, but only a double confession, never completely appeased; a double confession that only hope can hold together. According to the excellent phrase of André Néher, from his fine book *L'Essence du prophétisme*, a slice of nothingness separates the new creation from the old.[7] No *Aufhebung* [sublation] can suppress this deadly fault. This is why this double relation to history is profoundly betrayed when we apply the Stoic idea of providence to it and when the tension between narration and prophecy is assuaged in some teleological representation of the course of history.

Such a sliding over into teleology and the idea of providence would no doubt be unstoppable if we just leave the narrative discourse and the prophetic discourse regarding history face-to face-with each other. Reduced to this polarity, the idea of revelation indeed tends to be identified with the idea of God's design, the idea of a decreed plan that God has unmasked to his servants and prophets. But the polysemy and polyphony of revelation are not yet exhausted by this coupling of narration and prophecy.

There are at least three other modes of biblical religious discourse that cannot be inscribed within this polarity of narration and prophecy.

The first of these is the Torah, or instruction conveyed to Israel.

[7] André Néher, *L'Essence du prophétisme* (Paris: Presses Universitaires de France, 1955); reprinted as *Prophètes et prophéties: L'essence du prophétisme* (Paris: Payot, 2004).

Prescriptive Discourse

Broadly speaking, we may call this aspect of revelation its practical dimension. It corresponds to the symbolic expression "the will of God." If we may still speak of a design here, it is no longer in the sense of a plan about which thought may speculate, but in the sense of a prescription to be put into practice. But this idea of a revelation in the form of instruction is, in turn, full of pitfalls for the traditional understanding of revelation. In this regard, the translation, beginning with the Septuagint, of the word Torah by *nomos* or "law" is completely misleading. It leads us, in effect, to enclose the idea of an imperative from above within the idea of a divine law. If, moreover, we transcribe the idea of an imperative in terms of Kant's moral philosophy, we are more and more constrained to base the idea of revelation on that of heteronomy; that is, to express it in terms of submission to a higher, external commandment. That the idea of dependence is essential to the idea of revelation, is something I shall say in the second part of my remarks, but really to understand this originary dependence within the orders of speaking, willing, and being, we must first criticize the ideas of heteronomy and autonomy, both as taken together and as symmetrical to each other. Let us concentrate for the moment, however, on the idea of heteronomy. Nothing is more inadequate than this idea for making sense of what the term Torah has signified within Jewish experience. In order to do justice to the idea of a divine Torah, it does not even suffice to say that the Hebrew word Torah has a greater extension than what we call a moral commandment and that it is applied to the whole legislative system that the Old Testament tradition associated with Moses. By thus extending the commandment to all the domains of life of the community and the individual, whether moral, juridical, or cultic, we express only the amplitude of this phenomenon, without thereby really illuminating its specific nature.

Three points are worth emphasizing. First, it is not indifferent that the legislative texts of the Old Testament are placed in the mouth of Moses and within the narrative framework of the sojourn at Sinai. This means that this instruction is organically connected to the founding events symbolized by the exodus from

Egypt. In this regard, the introductory formula of the Decalogue constitutes an essential link connecting the story of the Exodus and the proclamation of the Law: "I am Yahweh, your God, who brought you out of the land of Egypt, out of the house of slavery" (Exod. 20:2). At the level of literary genres, this signifies that the legislative genre too is in a way included in the narrative genre. And this in turn signifies that the memory of deliverance qualifies the instruction in an intimate way. The Decalogue is the Law of a redeemed people. Such an idea is foreign to any simple concept of heteronomy.

This first comment leads to a second. The Law is one aspect of a much more concrete and encompassing relation than the relation between commanding and obeying, which characterizes the imperative. This relation is what the term "Covenant" itself translates imperfectly. It encompasses the ideas of Election and promise, as well as of threat and curse. The idea of the Covenant designates a whole complex of relations, running from the most fearful and meticulous obedience to the Law to casuistic interpretations, to intelligent meditation, to pondering in the heart, to the veneration of a joyous soul – as we shall see better with regard to the Psalms. The well-known Kantian respect for the law, in this regard, would only be one modality of what the Covenant signifies, and perhaps not the most significant one.

This space of variations opened by the Covenant for our ethical feelings suggests a third reflection. Despite the apparently invariable and apodictic character of the Decalogue, the Torah unfolds within a dynamism that we may well characterize as historical. By this we do not mean just the temporal development that historical criticism discerns in the redaction of these codes; an evolution of moral ideas may indeed be traced out from the first Decalogue to the Law of the Covenant, on the one hand, and from the Decalogue itself through the restatements and amplifications of the book of Deuteronomy to the new synthesis of the "Holiness Code" in the book of Leviticus and the legislation subsequent to Ezra, on the other. More important than this temporal development of the content of the Law is the transformation in the relationship between the faithful believer and the Law. Without falling into that old rut of opposing the legalistic and the prophetic, we may discover in the very teaching of the Torah an unceasing pulsation that turn by turn sets out the Law in terms of endlessly multiplying prescriptions and then draws it together, in the strong sense of the word, by summing it up in a set of commandments that retains only its being directed towards holiness. For example, the book of Deuteronomy proclaims long before the New Testament gospel: "You shall love Yahweh your God with all your heart, with all your soul, with all your strength. Let these words which I urge on you today be written on your heart" (6:5–6). This inscription on human hearts gave rise to the proclamation of a new covenant by some of the prophets, not in the sense of the proclamation of new precepts, but in the sense of a new relational quality as expressed precisely by the phrase "engraved on your hearts." Ezekiel wrote, "I will give them a new heart and I will put a new spirit in them; I will remove the heart of stone from their bodies and give them a heart of flesh..." (Ezek. 11:19). Without this pulsation in the Torah, we would not understand how Jesus could have, on the one hand, opposed the "traditions of the elders," which is to say, the multiplication and excessive load of commandments put forth by the Scribes and Pharisees, and, on the other hand, declared that in the Kingdom the Law would be fulfilled to its last iota. For Jesus, the Law and the Prophets were summed up in the Golden Rule from Deuteronomy: "So always treat others as you would like them to treat you: that is the meaning of the Law and the Prophets" (Matt. 7:12). In this sense, the Sermon on the Mount proclaims the same intention of perfection and holiness that runs through the ancient Law.

It is this intention that constitutes the ethical dimension of revelation. If we consider this instituting function of revelation, we see how inadequate the idea of heteronomy is for circumscribing the wealth of meaning included in the teaching of the Torah. We see also in what way the idea of revelation is enriched in turn. If we may still apply the idea of God's design for humans to it, it is no longer in the sense of a plan in which we could read past or future events, nor is it in terms of an immutable codification of every communal or individual practice. Rather it is the sense of a requirement for perfection that summons the will and makes a claim upon it. In the same way, if we may continue to speak of revelation as historical, it is not only in the sense that the trace of God may be read in the founding events of the past or in a coming conclusion to history, but in the sense that it orients the history of our practical actions and engenders the dynamics of our institutions.

Wisdom Discourse

But would this deepening of the Law beyond its being scattered among many precepts be perceived clearly if another dimension of revelation were not also recognized in its specificity? I mean, revelation as wisdom. Wisdom finds its literary expression in wisdom literature. But wisdom also surpasses every literary genre. At first glance, it appears as the art of living well, expert advice on the way to true happiness. It seems to turn the transcendent commandments of the Decalogue into tiny details, practical advice, only adding to the teaching of the Law a kind of lucidity without any illusions about human wickedness. But behind this somewhat shabby facade, we need to discern the great thrust of a reflection on existence that aims at the individual behind the people of the Covenant, and through the individual, every human being. In this way, wisdom overflows the framework of the Covenant, which is also the framework of the election of Israel and the promise made to Israel. The counsels of wisdom ignore the frontiers where any legislation appropriate to a single people stops, even if it is the elect people. It is not by chance that more than one sage in the biblical tradition was not a Jew. Wisdom intends every person in and through the Jew.

Its themes are those limit-situations spoken of by Karl Jaspers, those situations – including solitude, the fault, suffering, and death – where the woes and the grandeur of human beings confront each other. Hebraic wisdom interprets these situations as the annihilation of human beings and the incomprehensibility of God – as the silence and absence of God.

If the question of retribution is so pregnant here, it is so to the extent that the discordance between justice and happiness, cruelly emphasized by the triumph of the wicked, brings to light the overwhelming question of the sense or nonsense of existence. In this way, wisdom fulfills one of religion's fundamental functions, which is to bind together *ethos* and *cosmos*, the sphere of human action and the world's order. It does not do this by demonstrating that this conjunction is given in things, or by demanding that it be produced through our action. Rather it joins *ethos* and *cosmos* at the very point of their discordance: in suffering and, more precisely, in unjust suffering. Yet wisdom does not teach us how to avoid suffering, or how magically to deny it, or how to dissimulate it under an illusion. It teaches us how to endure, how to suffer suffering. It places suffering into a meaningful context by producing the active quality of suffering.

This is perhaps the most profound meaning of the book of Job, the best example of wisdom. If we take the *dénouement* of this book as our guide, could we not say that revelation, following the line of wisdom, is the intending of that horizon of meaning where a conception of the world and a conception of action merge into a new and active quality of suffering? The Eternal does not tell Job what order of reality justifies his suffering, nor what type of courage might vanquish it. The system of symbols wherein the revelation is conveyed is articulated beyond the point where models for a vision of the world and models for changing the world diverge. Model-of and model-for are rather the reverse sides of one indivisible prescriptive and descriptive symbolic order. This symbolic order can conjoin *cosmos* and *ethos* because it produces the *pathos* of actively assumed suffering. It is this pathos that is expressed in Job's final response:

> Then Job answered Yahweh, "I know that you can do all things, and that no purpose of yours can be thwarted. 'Who is this that hides counsel without knowledge?' Therefore I have uttered what I did not understand, things too wonderful for me, which I did not know. 'Hear, and I will speak; I will question you, and you declare to me.' I had heard of you by the hearing of the ear, but now my eye sees you; therefore I despise myself, and repent in dust and ashes." (Job 42:1–6)

What did Job "see"? Behemoth and Leviathan? The orders of creation? No. His questions about justice are left without an answer. But by repenting, though not of sin, for he is righteous, but by repenting for his supposition that existence does not make sense, Job presupposes an unsuspected meaning that cannot be transcribed by any speech or *logos* a human being may have at his disposal. This meaning has no other expression than the new quality that penitence confers on suffering. Hence, one can say in passing, it is not unrelated to what Aristotle speaks of as the tragic pathos that purifies the spectator of fear and pity.

We see at what point the notion of God's design – as may be suggested in different ways in each instance, it is true, by narrative, prophetic, and prescriptive discourse – is removed from any transcription in terms of a plan or program; in short, of finality and teleology. What is revealed is the possibility of hope "in spite of...." This possibility may still be expressed in the terms of a design, but it is of an unassignable design, a design that is God's secret.

We also see how the notion of revelation differs from one mode of discourse to another; especially when we pass from prophecy to wisdom. The prophet claims divine inspiration as guaranteeing what he says. The sage does nothing of the sort. He does not declare that his speech is the speech of another. But he does know that wisdom precedes him and that in a way it is through participation in wisdom that someone may be said to be wise. Nothing is further from the spirit of the sages than the idea of an autonomy of thinking, a humanism of the good life; in short, of a wisdom in the Stoic or Epicurean mode founded on the self-sufficiency of thought.

This is why wisdom is held to be a gift of God unlike the "knowledge of good and evil" promised by the Serpent. What is more, for the scribes following the Exile, Wisdom was personified as a transcendent feminine figure. She is a divine reality who has always existed and who will always exist. She lives with God and she has accompanied creation from its very beginning. Intimacy with Wisdom is not therefore to be distinguished from intimacy with God. By this detour wisdom rejoins prophecy. The objectivity of wisdom signifies the same thing as does the subjectivity of prophetic inspiration. This is why for the tradition the sage was held to be inspired by God just as the prophet was.

For the same reason, we can understand how prophecy and wisdom could converge in apocalyptic literature where, as we know, the notion of a revelation of the divine secrets is applied to "the last days." But such intermingling in no way prohibits the modes of religious discourse – and the aspects of revelation that correspond to them – from remaining distinct or from being held together only by a tie of pure analogy.

Hymnic Discourse

I do not want to end this brief survey of modes of biblical discourse without saying something about the lyric genre best exemplified by the Psalms. Hymns of praise, supplication, and thanksgiving constitute its three major genres. Clearly these are not marginal forms of religious discourse. The praise addressed to God's prodigious accomplishments in nature and history is not a movement of the heart that is added to narrative genre without any effect on its nucleus. Celebration in a way elevates the story and turns it into an invocation. Earlier I spoke of the example of the ancient creed from Deuteronomy – "A wandering Aramaean was my father, etc." In this sense, to retell the story is one aspect of celebration. Without a heart that sings the glory of God, perhaps we would not have the creation story, and certainly not the story of deliverance. And without the supplications in the psalms concerning suffering, would the moaning of the righteous find the path to invocation, even if it must lead to questioning and recrimination? Through supplication, the righteous person's protestations of innocence have as their opposite a Thou who may respond to his lamentation. In its conclusion, the book of Job has shown us how, instructed by wisdom, the knowledge of how to suffer is surpassed by the lyricism of supplication in the same way that narration is surpassed by the lyricism of praise. This movement toward the second person finds its fulfillment in the psalms of thanksgiving where the uplifted soul thanks someone. The invocation reaches its highest purity, its most disinterested expression, when the supplication, unburdened of every demand, is converted into gratitude. Thus under the three figures of praise, supplication, and thanksgiving human speech becomes invocation. It is addressed to God in the second person, without limiting itself to designating him in the third person as in narration, or to speaking in the first person in his name as in prophecy. I freely admit that the I–Thou relation may have been hypostasized to an excessive degree by what we might call the religious personalism of a Martin Buber or a Gabriel Marcel. This relation is really only constituted in the psalm, and above all in the psalm of supplication. We cannot say, therefore, that the idea of revelation is completely conveyed by this idea of a communication between two persons. Wisdom, we have seen, recognizes a hidden God who takes as his mask the anonymous and non-human course of events. We must therefore limit ourselves to noticing that in passing through the three positions of the system of first-person personal pronouns – I, you, he/she/it – the origin of revelation is designated in different modalities that are never completely identical with one another.

If we had to say in what sense the Psalter may be said to be revealed, it would certainly not be in the sense that its praise, supplication, and thanksgiving were placed in their disparate authors' mouths by God, but in the sense that the sentiments lyrically expressed there are formed by and conform to their object. Thanksgiving, supplication, and celebration are all engendered by what these movements of the heart allow to exist and, in that manner, to become manifest. The surpassing of *pathos*, which we have discerned in the movement of wisdom when it transforms suffering into knowing how to suffer, thus becomes in a way the theme of the Psalter. The word forms our feeling in the process of expressing it. And revelation is this very formation of our feelings that transcends their everyday, ordinary modalities.

If we now look back over the path we have covered, certain important conclusions are discernible.

First, I will reiterate my original affirmation that the analysis of religious discourse ought not to begin at the level of theological assertions such as "God exists," "God is immutable, omnipotent, etc." This propositional level constitutes a second-degree discourse, which is not conceivable without the incorporation of concepts borrowed from speculative philosophy. A hermeneutic of revelation must give priority to those modalities of discourse that are most originary within the language of a community of faith; consequently, those expressions by means of which the members of that community first interpret their experience for themselves and for others.

Second, these originary expressions are caught up in forms of discourse as diverse as narration, prophecy, legislative texts, wisdom sayings, hymns, supplications, and thanksgiving. The mistaken assumption here would be to take these forms of discourse as mere literary genres which ought to be neutralized so that we can extract their theological content. This presupposition is already at work in the reduction of the originary language of faith to its propositional content. To uproot this prejudice we must convince ourselves that the literary genres of the Bible do not constitute a rhetorical facade which it would be possible to pull down in order to reveal some thought content that is indifferent to its literary vehicle. But we will not get beyond this prejudice until we possess a *generative poetics* that would be for large works of literary composition what generative grammar is to the production of sentences following the characteristic rules of a given language. I will not, in this context, consider the implication of this thesis for literary criticism. It concerns the type of discourse that is always a work of a certain genre, i.e., a work produced as narration, as prophecy, as legislation, etc. Instead, I will proceed directly to what concerns our inquiry about revelation. To be brief, I will say that the confession of faith expressed in the biblical documents is directly modulated by the forms of discourse wherein it is expressed. This is why the difference between narrative and prophecy, so characteristic of the Old Testament, is per se theologically significant. Not just any theology may be attached to the story form, only a theology that celebrates Yahweh as the great liberator. The theology of the Pentateuch, if the word "theology" itself is not premature here, is a theology homogeneous with the structure of the story; i.e., a theology in the form of a history of salvation. But this theology is not a system to the extent that, at the same level of radicality or originariness, prophetic discourse undoes the assurance founded on the recitation and repetition of the founding events. The motif of the "Day of Yahweh" – a day of mourning, not of joy – is not a rhetorical motif that we can simply eliminate. It is a constitutive element of the prophetic theology. The same thing applies to the Torah, as well as to the spiritual tenor of the hymn. What announces itself there is in each instance qualified by the form of the announcement. The religious "saying" is constituted in the interplay between story and prophecy, history and legislation, legislation and wisdom, and finally wisdom and lyricism.

Third, if the forms of religious discourse are so pregnant with meaning, the notion of revelation can no longer be formulated in the uniform and monotonous fashion that we presuppose when we speak of *the* biblical revelation. If we place in parentheses the properly theological work of synthesis and systematization that presupposes the neutralization of the primitive forms of discourse and the transference of every religious content onto the plane of the assertion or proposition, we then arrive at a polysemic and polyphonic concept of revelation. Earlier I spoke of such a concept as analogical. Now I want to explain this analogy. It proceeds from a reference term: prophetic discourse. There, revelation signifies inspiration from a first person to a first person. The word "prophet" implies the notion of a person who is driven by God to speak, and who does speak to the people in God's name and in his own name. If we do not catch sight of the analogical bond between the other forms of religious discourse and prophetic discourse, we generalize in univocal fashion the concept of inspiration derived from the prophetic genre and assume that God spoke to the redactors of the sacred books just as he spoke to the prophets. The Scriptures are then said to have been written by the Holy Spirit. We are then inclined to construct a uniform theology of the double divine and human author, wherein God is posited as the formal cause and the writer is posited as the instrumental cause of these texts. However, through this generalization, we do not render justice to those aspects of revelation that are not reducible to being synonymous with the double voice of the prophet. The narrative genre invited us to displace onto the recounted events that revealing light which proceeds from their founding value and their instituting function. The narrator is a prophet, but only inasmuch as the events that generate meaning are brought to language. In this way, a less subjective concept than that of inspiration is roughed out. In a similar manner, the nuances of revelation derived from the prescriptive force of instruction, the illuminating capacity of the wisdom saying, and the quality of lyrical pathos in the hymn are connected to those forms of discourse. Inspiration, then, designates the coming to language of this prescriptive force, this illuminating capacity, and this lyrical pathos, but only as analogous to one another. We over-psychologize revelation if we fall back on the notion of scripture as dictated in a literal fashion. It is the force of what is spoken of that moves the writer. That something requires to be said is what the Nicene Creed analogically signifies by the expression, "I believe in the Holy Spirit... who spoke through the prophets." Yet we do not have, at least in the West, an appropriate theology that does not psychologize the Holy Spirit. To discover the objective dimension of revelation would be to contribute indirectly to this non-psychologizing theology of the Holy Spirit, which would be a genuine *pneumatology*.

Allow me now to draw a final conclusion. If one thing may be said unequivocally about all the analogical forms of revelation, it is that in none of its modalities may revelation be included in and dominated by knowledge. In this regard the idea of something *secret* is the limit-idea of revelation. The idea of revelation is a twofold idea. The God who reveals himself is a hidden God and hidden things belong to him.

The confession that God is infinitely above human thoughts and speech, that he guides us without our comprehending his ways, that the fact that human beings are an enigma to themselves which even obscures the clarity that God communicates to us – this confession belongs to the idea of revelation. The one who reveals himself is also the one who conceals himself. And in this regard nothing is as significant as the episode of the burning bush in Exodus 3:13–15. Tradition has quite rightly named this episode the revelation of the divine *name*. For this name is precisely *unnameable*, inasmuch as to know God's name is to have power over him through an invocation whereby the god invoked becomes a manipulable thing; the name confided to Moses is that of the being who human beings cannot really name; that is, hold within the discretion of their language.

> But Moses said to God, "If I come to the Israelites and say to them, 'The God of your ancestors has sent me to you,' and they ask me, 'What is his name?' what shall I say to them?" God said to Moses, "I am who I am," He said further, "Thus you shall say to the Israelites, 'I am has sent me to you.'" (Exodus 3:13–14)

Thus the appellation Yahweh – *he is* – is not a name that defines God, but one that signifies, one that signifies the act of deliverance. The text continues:

> God also said to Moses, "Thus you shall say to the Israelites, 'The Lord, the God of your ancestors, the God of Abraham, the God of Isaac, and the God of Jacob, has sent me to you.' This is my name forever, and this my title for all generations." (Exodus 3: 15)

In this way the historical revelation – signified by the names of Abraham, Isaac, and Jacob – depends on the secret of the name, in that the hidden God proclaims himself as the meaning of the founding events. The revelation takes place between the secret and the revealed.

I am well aware that tradition has interpreted the *Ehyeh asher ehyeh* in the sense of a positive, ontological assertion, following the Septuagint translation: "I am who I am." Far from protecting the secret, this translation opened up an affirmative noetics of God's absolute being that could subsequently be transcribed into Neoplatonic and Augustinian ontology, and then into Aristotelian and Thomist metaphysics. In this way, the theology of the name could pass over into an onto-theology capable of taking up and bracketing the theology of history, and in which the meaning of narration and of prophecy was sublimated and rationalized. The dialectic of the hidden God who reveals himself – the core dialectic of revelation – was thereby dissipated into the knowledge of being and of providence. To say that the God who reveals himself is a hidden God is, on the contrary, to confess that revelation can never constitute a body of truths that an institution may boast of or take pride in possessing. So to dissipate the massive opacity of the concept of revelation is also at the same time to overthrow every totalitarian form of authority which might claim to withhold the revealed truth. In this way, my first reflections end by returning to the point where we began.

The Response of a Hermeneutic Philosophy

What is philosophy's task in response to the *claim* which proceeds from a concept of revelation as differentiated as the one I have just outlined? Claim – *Anspruch* – can signify two different things: undue and unacceptable *pretension* or an *appeal* that does not force one to accept its message. I want to understand claim in this second sense. But the reversal that comes through listening to this claim can be produced only if, in symmetry with the critique of an opaque and authoritarian concept of revelation, philosophy proceeds in its own self-understanding to a critique of its own *pretension*, which causes it to understand the appeal of revelation as an unacceptable claim opposed to it. If the unacceptable pretentious claim of the idea of revelation is in the final analysis that of a *sacrificium intellectus* and of a total heteronomy under the verdict of the magisterium, the opposed pretentious claim of philosophy is its claim to a complete transparency of truth and a total autonomy of the thinking subject. When these two pretensions simply confront each other, they constitute an unbridgeable canyon between what some call the "truths of faith" and others call the "truths of reason."

I want to direct my remarks to a critique of this double pretension of philosophy, with the idea that at the end of such undertaking the apparently unreasonable claim of revelation might be better understood as a nonconstraining appeal.

But before undertaking this critique, allow me to list which ways I will not follow. First, I set apart from my own proposal the project of a rational theology, which other philosophers whom I respect believe to be possible in practice. If I do not seek to restate the proofs for the existence of God, and if I do not inquire into the relation of concordance or of subordination that might exist between two orders of truth, it is as much for reasons based on the interpretation of biblical revelation given above as for the idea of philosophy that I make use of. My remarks in part one essentially tried to carry the idea of revelation back to a more originary level than that of theology, the level of its fundamental discourse. This discourse is established close to human experience and life. It is therefore in experiences more fundamental than any onto-theological articulation that I will seek the features of a truth capable of being spoken of in terms of manifestation rather than verification, as well as the features of a self-awareness wherein the subject would free himself of the arrogance of consciousness. These are those cardinal experiences, as language brings them to expression, that can enter into resonance or consonance with the modes of revelation brought to language by the most primitive expressions of the faith of Israel and of early Christianity. This homology in no way requires that philosophy know God. The word "God," it seems to me, belongs first to the pre-theological expressions of faith. God is The One who is proclaimed, invoked, questioned, supplicated, and thanked. The meaning of the term "God" circulates among all these modes of discourse, but in escaping each one of them, according to the vision of the burning bush, it is in a way their vanishing point.

The experiences of manifestation and of dependence therefore need not be referred to God – and still less serve to prove God's existence – in order to remain in resonance with those modes of experience and expression that, by themselves, signify God in the first place.

There is another way that I also will not follow: the way of an existentialism based on the wretchedness of the human condition, where philosophy provides the questions and religion the answers. No doubt, an apologetic based on the wretchedness of existence does satisfy the existential conditions imposed by the level of discourse we attained in our first section. Furthermore, it numbers among its practitioners such worthy names as Pascal and Tillich. But its apologetic character is suspect inasmuch as it is apologetic. If God speaks by the prophets, the philosopher does not have to justify this Word, but rather to set out the horizon of significance wherein it may be heard. Such work has nothing to do with apologetics. Furthermore, recourse to anxiety, to a sense of something lacking, is no less suspect. Bonhoeffer has said all that needs to be said against the God of the gaps, whether it be a question of explaining things or of understanding humanity. The philosophy of misery, even if one is not a Marxist, remains the misery of philosophy.

This is why I prefer to turn toward some *structures of interpretation* of human experience, to discern there those features through which something has always been comprehensible under the idea of revelation understood in an a-religious sense of the term. It is this comprehension that may enter into consonance with the non-constraining appeal of biblical revelation.

My analysis will consist of two parts, corresponding to the twofold claim of philosophical discourse to transparent objectivity and subjective autonomy. The first remarks will be directed toward the space of the manifestation of things, the second toward that understanding of themselves that humans gain when they allow themselves to be governed by what is manifested and said. These two dimensions of the problem correspond to the two major objections that are usually directed against the very principle of a revealed word. According to the first objection, any idea of revelation violates the idea of objective truth as measured by the criteria of empirical verification and falsification. According to the second objection, the idea of revelation denies the autonomy of the thinking subject inscribed within the idea of a consciousness completely in control of itself. The double meditation I propose will address in turn these claims to transparency founded on a concept of truth as adequation and verification, and to autonomy founded on the concept of a sovereign consciousness.

If I begin with the former point, it is for a fundamental reason, namely, that the conquest of a new concept of truth as *manifestation* – and in this sense as revelation – demands the recognition of our real dependence which is in no way synonymous with heteronomy. The choice of this order of discussion also is in perfect agreement with the critique I offered in my first part of the subjectivism and psychologism engendered by a certain inflation of the idea of inspiration. I said, in effect, let us rather first look on the side of those events that make history or that are part of the impending future. Let us look on the side of the prescriptive force of the law of perfection; toward the objective quality of the feelings – the pathos – articulated by the hymn. In the same way, I now say, let us allow the space of the manifestation of things to be, before we turn toward the consciousness of the thinking and speaking subject.

The World of the Text and the New Being

My first investigation, into what I will call the space of the manifestation of things, takes place within precise limits. I will not speak of our experience of being-in-the-world, beginning from a phenomenology of perception as may be found in the works of Husserl and Merleau-Ponty, nor in terms of a phenomenology of care or preoccupation as can be found in Heidegger's *Being and Time* – although I believe that they may be connected by means of the detour I propose. Instead I will begin directly from the *manifestation of the world by the text and by scripture.*

This approach may seem overly limited, insofar as it proceeds through the narrow defile of one cultural fact, the fact that it is limited to cultures which possess books. But it will seem less limited once we have understood what enlargement of our experience of the world results from the existence of such cultures based on books. Moreover, by choosing this angle of attack, we immediately establish a correspondence with the fact that the claim of revealed speech reaches us today through writings to be interpreted. Those religions which refer back to Abraham – Judaism, Christianity, and Islam – are in their different ways, and they are often very different ways, religions of the Book. It is therefore appropriate to inquire into the particular revelatory function attached to certain modes of scripture that I will place under the heading *poetics*, in a sense I shall explain in a moment. In brief, under the category of poetics, philosophical analysis encounters those features of revelation that may correspond with or respond to the nonconstraining appeal of biblical revelation.

To introduce this idea of a revelatory function of poetic discourse, I will draw upon three preparatory concepts (which I have examined at greater length in my other writings on hermeneutics).

The first one is the very concept of writing. We underestimate the phenomenon of writing if we reduce it to the mere material fixation of actual speech. Writing stands in a specific relation to what is said. It produces a form of discourse that is immediately autonomous with regard to its author's intention. And in this autonomy is already contained everything that I will call in a moment, following Hans-Georg Gadamer, the *issue* of the text, which is removed from the finite intentional horizon of the author. In other words, thanks to writing, the world of the text can break through the world of the author. This emancipation with regard to the author has its parallel on the side of whoever receives the text. The autonomy of the text also transports this reader beyond the finite horizon of its original audience.

The second preparatory concept is that of the *work*. By this I mean the shaping of discourse through the operation of literary genres such as narration, fiction, the essay, etc. By producing discourse as a work taking up this or that genre, the composition codes assign to works of discourse that unique configuration we call a style. This shaping of the work concurs with the phenomenon of writing in externalizing and objectifying the text into what one literary critic has called a "verbal icon."[8]

The third preparatory concept points in the same direction and goes a bit further. It is what I call the *world of the text*. By this

[8] W. K. Wimsatt, *The Verbal Icon: Studies in the Meaning of Poetry* (Lexington: University of Kentucky Press, 1954).

I mean that what is finally to be understood in a text is not the author or his presumed intention, nor is it the immanent structure or structures of the text, but rather the sort of world intended beyond the text as its reference. In this regard, the alternative "either the intention or the structure" is vain. For the *reference* of the text – what I call the issue of the text or the world of the text – is neither of these. Intention and structure have to do with its "sense," the world of the text designates the reference of the work of discourse, not *what* is said, but *about what* it is said. Hence the issue of the text is the object of hermeneutics. And the issue of the text is the world the text unfolds before itself.

On this threefold basis – autonomy through writing, externalization by means of the work, and the reference to a world – I will construct the analysis, central to our discussion of the revelatory function of poetic discourse, of the *revelatory* function of *poetic* discourse. I have not until now introduced this category of poetics, which does not designate one of the literary genres discussed in the first part of my presentation, but rather the totality of these genres – prophetic, narrative, legislative, wisdom, hymnic – inasmuch as they exercise a referential function that differs from the *descriptive* referential function of ordinary language and above all of scientific discourse. Hence I will speak of the poetic function of discourse in general and not of a poetic genre or a mode of poetic discourse. This function, in turn, is defined precisely in terms of its referential function. What is this referential function?

As a first approximation, the poetic function indicates the obliterating of the referential function, at least if we identify it with the capacity to describe familiar objects of perception or the objects which science alone determines by means of its standards of measurement. Poetic discourse suspends this *descriptive* function. It does not directly augment our knowledge of objects. From here, it is only a short step to saying that in poetry language turns back on itself to celebrate itself. But if we say this, we accede too quickly to the positivist presupposition that only empirical knowledge is objective knowledge, because it is verifiable. We do not notice that we uncritically accept a certain concept of truth defined as *adequation* to real objects and as submitted to a criterion of empirical *verification*. That language in its poetic function abolishes the type of reference characteristic of such descriptive discourse, and along with it, the reign of truth as adequation and the very definition of truth in terms of verification, is not to be doubted. The question is whether this suspension or abolition of a referential function of the first degree is not the negative condition for the liberating of a more primitive, more originary referential function, which may be called a second-order reference only because discourse whose function is *descriptive* has usurped the first rank in daily life, and has been supported in this regard by modern science. My deepest conviction is that poetic language alone restores to us that *participation-in* or *belonging-to* an order of things that precedes our capacity to oppose ourselves to things taken as objects opposed to a subject. The function of poetic discourse is to bring about this emergence of a depth-structure of belonging-to amid the ruins of descriptive discourse. Once again, this function is in no way to be identified with poetry, understood as something opposed to prose and defined by a certain affinity of sense, rhythm, image, and sound. I am first defining the poetic function in a negative manner, following Roman Jakobson, as the inverse of the referential function, understood in a narrowly descriptive sense, then in a positive way, as what in my book on metaphor I call the metaphorical reference.[9] Through this metaphorical reference, we do not say what things are, but rather speak of them as we see them. In this regard, the most extreme paradox is that when language most enters into fiction – e.g., when a poet forges the plot of a tragedy – it most speaks truth because it redescribes reality so well known that it is taken for granted in terms of the new features of this plot. *Fiction* and *redescription*, then, go hand in hand. Or, to speak like Aristotle in his *Poetics*, the *muthos* is the way to true *mimesis*, which is not slavish imitation, or a copy, or mirror image, but a transposition or metamorphosis – or, as I suggest, a redescription. This conjunction of fiction and redescription, of *muthos* and *mimesis*, constitutes the referential function by means of which I would define the poetic dimension of language.

In turn, this poetic function conceals a dimension of revelation in a nonreligious, nontheistic, and nonbiblical sense of the word – but one capable of entering into resonance with one or the other of the aspects of biblical revelation. How is this so?

[9] Paul Ricoeur, *The Rule of Metaphor: Multi-Disciplinary Studies in the Creation of Meaning in Language,* trans. Robert Czerny with Kathleen McLaughlin and John Costello, SJ (Toronto: University of Toronto Press, 1977).

In the following manner: First, the poetic function recapitulates in itself the three preparatory concepts of the autonomy of the text, the externality of the work, and the transcendence of the world of the text. By means of these three features, an order of things shows itself, which does not belong to either the author or the original audience. But to these three features the poetic function adds a split reference, by means of which emerges the Atlantis submerged in the network of objects submitted to the domination of our preoccupations. It is the emergence of this primordial ground of our existence, of the originary horizon of our being-there, that is the *revelatory* function which is coextensive with the poetic function.

But why call it *revelatory*? Because, through all the features it recapitulates and by what it adds, the poetic function incarnates a concept of truth that escapes the definition in terms of adequation, as well as the criteria of falsification and verification. Here truth no longer means verification, but manifestation, that is, letting what shows itself be. What shows itself is in each instance a proposed world, a world I may inhabit and wherein I can project my ownmost possibilities.[10] It is in this sense of manifestation that language in its poetic function is a vehicle of revelation.

By using the word "revelation" in such a nonbiblical and even nonreligious way, do we abuse the word? I do not believe so. Our analysis of the biblical concept of revelation has prepared for us a first-degree analogical use of the term and here we are led to a second-degree analogy. The first-degree analogy was assured by the role of the first analogue, prophetic discourse, with its implication of another voice behind the prophet's voice. This meaning of the first analogue was communicated to all the other modes of discourse to the extent that they could be said to be inspired. But we also saw that this analogy with reference to the *princeps* discourse, that of prophecy, did not do justice to the specific character of each of the other modes of discourse, above all narrative discourse, where what is said or recounted, the generative historical

---

[10] In the discussion included in *La Révélation*, Ricoeur states that "it is the world of the text that projects the 'Kingdom of God,' a 'new being.' This proposed existence, life, world, Kingdom, seems to me capable of engendering a practice, a practice of reading first of all, of knowing how to hear the word speaking in the text" (210).

event, came to language through the narration. It is this primacy of what is said over the inspiration of the narrator that the philosophical concept of revelation leads, by means of a second analogy, which is no longer that of *inspiration*, but that of *manifestation*.

This new analogy invites us to place the originary expressions of biblical faith under the sign of the poetic function of language. Not to deprive them of a referent, but to put them under the law of split reference that characterizes the poetic function. Religious discourse is poetic in all the senses we have spoken of. Being written down as scripture removes it from the finite horizon of its authors and its first audience. The style of its literary genres gives it the externality of a work. And the intended implicit reference of each text opens onto a world, the biblical world, or rather the multiple worlds unfolded before the book through its narration, prophecy, prescriptions, wisdom, and hymns. The proposed world that, in biblical language, is called a new world, a new Covenant, the Kingdom of God, is the "issue" of the biblical text unfolded in front of this text. Finally, and above all, this "issue" of the biblical text is indirectly intended beyond the suspension of descriptive, didactic, and informative discourse. And this abolition of the reference to objects that we can manipulate allows the world of our originary rootedness to appear. Just as the world of poetic texts opens its way across the ruins of the intraworldly objects of everyday existence and of science, so too the new being projected by the biblical text opens its way across the world of ordinary experience and in spite of the closed nature of that experience. The power to project this new world is the power of breaking through and of an opening.

In this way, the a-religious sense of revelation helps us to restore the concept of biblical revelation to its full dignity.[11] It

---

[11] "I confirm that I did not intend to present a theology of revelation, but a philosophy of revelation. That means, listening to a word that is a source for me, I try to approximate this word with the internal resources of philosophy, which do not include revealed elements. I believe this duality must be maintained; I said so at the start of my presentation. Philosophy, to me, does not have the task of speaking about God. On the contrary, philosophy is human, worldly. But the philosophical act can provide an approximation of what is signified in revelation through the very movement of dispossessing and setting aside the ego" (*La Révélation*, 228–9).

delivers us from psychologizing interpretations of the inspiration of the Scriptures, in the sense of their words having been whispered in the writers' ears. If the Bible may be said to be revealed, this must refer to what it speaks of, to the new being it unfolds before us. Revelation is a feature of the biblical world.

Yet if this a-religious sense of revelation has such a corrective value, it does not for all that include the religious meaning of revelation. There is a homology between them, but nothing allows us to derive the specific feature of religious language – namely, that its referent "God" circulates among prophecy, narration, prescription, wisdom, and psalms, coordinating these diverse and partial forms of discourse by giving them a vanishing point and an index of incompleteness. Biblical hermeneutics is in turn one regional hermeneutics within a general hermeneutics and a unique hermeneutic that makes use of philosophical hermeneutics as its organon. It is one particular case, in that the Bible is one of the great poems of existence. A unique case because all its partial forms of discourse are referred to by that Name which is the point of intersection and the vanishing point of all our discourse about God, the name of the Unnameable. This is the paradoxical homology that the category of the *world of the text* establishes between revelation in the broad sense of poetic discourse and in the specifically biblical sense.

Mediating Reflection and Testimony

We may now return to the second pretension that philosophy opposes to the claim of revealed truth. This is its claim to autonomy. It is founded on the concept of a subject who is master of his thoughts. This idea of a consciousness that posits itself in positing its contents undoubtedly constitutes the strongest resistance to any idea of revelation, not only in the specific sense of the religions of the book, but also in the larger, more global sense that we have just connected to the poetic function of discourse.

I will proceed here with regard to the second part of my analysis in the same manner as for the first. Instead of taking up the question of the autonomy of consciousness in its most general sense, I will attempt to focus the debate on a central concept of self-awareness, which is capable of corresponding to one of the major features of the idea of revelation brought to light by our analysis of biblical discourse. This central category will occupy a place comparable to that of poetic discourse in relation to the "objective" aspect of philosophical discourse. This category, which to me best signifies the self-implication of the subject in his discourse, is that of *testimony*. Besides having a corresponding term on the side of the idea of revelation, it is the most appropriate concept for making us understand what a thinking subject formed by and conforming to poetic discourse might be.

But before undertaking a properly philosophical reflection on the category of testimony, I will, here once again, call on some preparatory concepts, which I have explicated at greater length in my other work on hermeneutics.

First, the concept of the *cogito* as mediated by a universe of signs. Without yet appealing to the mediation by means of the text, the written work, I would like to recall in the most general terms what primary dependence upholds a subject who, contrary to Descartes' assertion, does not have at his disposal an immediate intuition of his existence and his essence as a thinking being. From *The Symbolism of Evil* on, I have perceived this constitutional infirmity of Descartes' *cogito*. To pierce the secret of the evil will, we must take the detour of a semantics and an exegesis applied to those symbols and myths in which the millenary experience of the confession of evil is deposited. But it was with *Freud and Philosophy* that I decisively broke away from the illusions of consciousness as the blind spot of reflection.[12] The case of the symbolism of evil is not an exception, one tributary of the gloomy experience of evil. All reflection is mediated. There is no immediate self-consciousness. The first truth, I said, that of the "I think, I am," "remains as abstract and empty as it is invincible: it has to be 'mediated' by the ideas, actions, works, institutions, and monuments that objectify it. It is in these objects, in the widest sense of the word, that the Ego must lose and find itself. We can say, in a somewhat paradoxical sense, that a philosophy of reflection is not a philosophy of consciousness, if by consciousness we mean immediate self-consciousness."[13]

---

[12] Paul Ricoeur, *Freud and Philosophy: An Essay on Interpretation*, trans. Denis Savage (New Haven: Yale University Press, 1970).
[13] Ibid., 43.

Adopting the language of Jean Nabert – as I will do again in my analysis of testimony – I defined reflection by "the appropriation of our effort to exist and of our desire to be, through the works which bear witness to that effort and desire."[14] In this way, I included testimony within the structure of reflection without as yet having determined the importance of this implication. At least I saw that "the positing or emergence of this effort or desire is not only devoid of all intuition but is evidenced only by works whose meaning remains doubtful and revocable."[15] This is why reflection had to include interpretation; that is: "the results, methods, and presuppositions of all the sciences that try to decipher and interpret the signs of man."[16]

The second preparatory concept is that of participation or "belonging-to" [*appartenance*], which I borrow from Gadamer's *Truth and Method*.[17] For me, the conquest of this concept marked the end of a difficult struggle with Husserlian idealism which was not yet broached by the preceding avowal of the mediated character of reflection. It was still necessary to call into question Husserl's scientific ideal, especially in the sense of a "final justification" or a "self-founding" of the transcendental ego, to discover in the *finite* ontological condition of self-understanding the unsurpassable limit of this scientific ideal. The ultimate condition of any enterprise of justification or of grounding is that it is always preceded by a relation that already carries it:

> Is this a relation to the object? This is precisely what it is not. The aspect of Husserlian idealism is that hermeneutics questions first the way in which the immense and unsurpassable discovery of intentionality is couched in a conceptuality that weakens its scope, namely, the conceptuality of the subject-object relation.... The first declaration of hermeneutics is to say that the problematic of objectivity presupposes a prior relation of inclusion that encompasses the allegedly autonomous subject and the allegedly adverse

14 Ibid., 46.
15 Ibid.
16 Ibid.
17 Hans-Georg Gadamer, *Truth and Method*, 2nd, rev. edn, rev. and trans. Joel Weinsheimer and Donald G. Marshall (New York: Crossroad, 1991).

object. This inclusive or encompassing relation is what I call belonging.[18]

What is undercut here is the primacy of reflection that, at first, was left out of the critique of the illusions of consciousness. Reflection does not disappear. That would make no sense at all. But its status is to be always a "second-order reflection," to speak like Gabriel Marcel. It corresponds to that *distanciation* without which we would never become conscious of belonging to a world, a culture, a tradition. It is the critical moment, originally bound to the consciousness of belonging-to, that confers its properly historical character on this consciousness. For even a tradition only becomes such under the condition of a distance that distinguishes the belonging-to proper to a human being from the simple inclusion of a thing as a part of a whole. Reflection is never first, never constituting – it arrives unexpectedly like a "crisis" within an experience that bears us, and it constitutes us as the subject of the experience.

The third preparatory concept is caught sight of in the prolongation of this dialectic of belonging-to and distanciation. It makes more precise our mode of belonging to a culture like our own where the signs are texts, i.e., writings and works arising out of distinct literary genres. This third concept corresponds, in the "subjective" order, to the concept of the world of the text in the "objective" order. You will recall my insistence on defining the hermeneutic task not in terms of the author's intention, supposedly hidden behind the text, but in terms of the quality of being-in-the-world unfolded in front of the text, as the reference of the text. The "subjective" concept that corresponds to that of the world of the text is the concept of appropriation. By this, I mean the very act of *understanding oneself in front of the text*. This act is the exact counterpart of the autonomy of writing and the externalization of the work. It in no way is intended to make the reader correspond with the mind of the author. For it does not respond to the author, but to the sense and reference of the work. Its other is the issue of the text, the world of the work.

[18] "Phenomenology and Hermeneutics," in Paul Ricoeur, *From Text to Action: Essays in Hermeneutics II*, trans. Kathleen Blamey and John B. Thompson (Evanston: Northwestern University Press, 1991), 29–30.

This third preparatory concept marks the final defeat of the pretension of consciousness to set itself up as the standard of meaning. To understand oneself in front of the text is not

> A question of imposing upon the text our finite capacity for understanding, but of exposing ourselves to the text and receiving from it an enlarged self, which would be the proposed existence corresponding in the most suitable way to the world proposed. So understanding is quite different from a constitution of which the subject would possess the key. In this respect, it would be more correct to say that the *self* is constituted by the issue of the text.[19]

How, you might ask, are these three concepts of mediated reflection, belonging-to or second-order reflection, and finally appropriation as self-understanding in front of the text preparatory concepts? They are preparatory insofar as they bring about, on a purely epistemological, even a methodological level, consciousness's *abandoning of its pretension* to constitute every signification in and beginning from itself. This abandonment [*dessaisissement*] takes place on the very terrain of the historical and hermeneutical sciences, at the very heart of the problematic of understanding, where the tradition of Romanticist hermeneutics had thought to establish the reign of subjectivity. It is the final consequence of a critique of Romanticist hermeneutics, at the end of which the concept of the *world of the text* has taken the place of the *author's intention*.

Perhaps you have begun to realize how the pretension of consciousness to constitute itself is the most formidable obstacle to the idea of revelation. In this regard, the transcendental idealism of a Husserl contains implicitly the same atheistic consequences as does the idealism of consciousness of a Feuerbach. If consciousness *posits itself*, it must be the "subject" and the divine must be the "predicate," and it can only be through an alienation subsequent to this power of self-production that God is projected as the fictitious "subject" for whom the human being becomes the "predicate." The hermeneutical movement I have just traced

[19] "The Hermeneutical Function of Distanciation," in ibid., 88 (trans. altered).

brings about a conversion diametrically opposed to that of Feuerbach. Where consciousness posits itself as the origin of meaning, hermeneutics brings about the "abandonment" of this pretension. This "abandonment" – it must be said – is the converse of Feuerbach's critique of alienation.

But such a consequence can only be anticipated and glimpsed on the unique basis of a hermeneutic where self-understanding is the reply to notions as strictly "literary" as those of the text, the work, and the world of the text. It is precisely the function of the category of testimony – the central category of this second phase of our philosophical inquiry – to demolish a bit further the fortress of consciousness. It introduces the dimension of *historical contingency* which is lacking in the concept of the world of the work, which is deliberately ahistorical or transhistorical. It directly assaults therefore one fundamental characteristic of the idea of autonomy; namely, not making the internal itinerary of consciousness depend on external events. As Jean Nabert puts it in his *Essai sur le mal*, "Do we have the right to invest one moment of history with an absolute characteristic?"[20] You may recall that this is what also scandalized Karl Jaspers in the phenomenon of religion. According to Jaspers, "philosophical faith" ought to eliminate the arbitrary privileging of this or that moment of humanity's spiritual history. This refusal of historical contingency therefore constitutes one of the most dug-in defenses of the claim to autonomy. A meditation on the category of testimony is meant to confront this refusal.

Few philosophers, to my knowledge, have attempted to integrate the category of testimony into philosophical reflection. Most have either ignored it or abandoned it to the realm of faith. One exception is Jean Nabert in his book *Le Désir de Dieu*.[21] I want to draw on this work to show how this category governs the abandonment of, the letting go of the absolute claim to self-consciousness, and how it occupies on the "subjective" side of a hermeneutic of revelation a strategic position similar to that of the category of *poetics* on the "objective" side.

[20] Jean Nabert, *Essai sur le mal* (Paris: Presses Universitaires de France, 1955), 148. – Ricoeur's note.
[21] Jean Nabert, *Le Désir de Dieu* (Paris: Éditions Montaigne, 1966; Cerf 1996).

Recourse to testimony occurs in a philosophy of reflection at the moment when such a philosophy renounces the pretension of consciousness to constitute itself. For example, Jean Nabert comes to the place of testimony at that point of his itinerary where concrete reflection exerts itself to rejoin what he calls that originary affirmation that constitutes me more than I constitute it. This "originary affirmation"

> has all the characteristics of an absolute affirmation of the absolute, but it is unable to go beyond a purely internal act, incapable of outwardly expressing itself, or of even inwardly maintaining itself. Originary affirmation has something of the indefinitely inaugural about it, and that only concerns the idea which the ego makes of itself. For a philosophy of reflection, this originary affirmation is in no way one of our experiences. Although numerically identical to real [*réelle*] consciousness in everyone, it is the act that accomplishes the negation of those limitations which affect an individual's destiny. It is letting go [*dépouillement*].[22]

In one sense, this letting go is still part of the reflective order. It is both an ethical and a speculative act. It means renouncing not only the empirical objects ordered by reason, but also those transcendental objects of metaphysics that might still provide a basis for thinking the unconditioned. Consequently, this letting go takes up and continues the Kantian meditation on the transcendental illusion as presented in the section on "Dialectic" in the first *Critique*. It could also be expressed by the language of the *Enneads* where Plotinus exclaims *Aphele panta* – "abolish everything."

It is precisely this movement of letting go that carries reflection to the encounter with contingent signs of the absolute which the absolute, in its generosity, allows to appear. This avowal of the absolute can no longer be Kantian (nor, no doubt, Plotinian), for Kantian philosophy would incline us to look only for *examples*, or *symbols*, not for *testimonies*, understood as accounts of an *experience* of the absolute. In an example, the case is effaced under the rule and the person is effaced under the law. An abstraction

[22] Paul Ricoeur, "The Hermeneutics of Testimony," in Ricoeur, *Essays on Biblical Interpretation*, ed. Lewis S. Mudge (Philadelphia: Fortress Press, 1980), 120 (trans. altered). – Ricoeur's note.

takes the place of the originary affirmation, the abstraction of the norm. But the encounter with evil in the experience of what cannot be justified does not allow us the leisure to grant our veneration to the sublimity of the moral order. The unjustifiable constrains us to let go of this very veneration. Only those events, acts, and persons that attest that the unjustifiable is overcome here and now can reopen the path toward originary affirmation. As for the symbol, it is no less feeble than the example with regard to the unjustifiable. Its inexhaustible richness of meaning no doubt gives it a consistency that the example lacks. But its historicity places it at the mercy of the work of interpretation that may dissipate it too quickly into too ideal forms of meaning. Only "testimony that is singular in each instance confers the sanction of reality on ideas, ideals, and ways of being that the symbol depicts to us and which we uncover as our ownmost possibilities."[23]

In this way, testimony, better than either an example or a symbol, places reflection before the paradox, which the pretension of consciousness makes a scandal. I mean that a moment of history is invested with an absolute character. This paradox ceases to be a scandal as soon as the wholly internal movement of letting go, of abandoning the claim to found consciousness accepts being led by and ruled by the interpretation of external signs that the absolute gives of itself. And the hermeneutic of testimony consists wholly in the convergence of these two movements, these two exegeses: the exegesis of self and the exegesis of external signs.

Testimony, on the one side, is able to be taken up internally in reflection thanks to several dialectical features that arouse and call for this reflective repetition in us.

It first proposes the dialectic of its object, which is both an event and a meaning, similar to what we spoke of in part one with regard to the narration of the founding events of the history of Israel. For the Hebraic confession of faith, the event and its meaning immediately coincide. It is the moment that Hegel called the moment of absolute or revealed religion. But this moment of fusion of event and meaning fades away. Its appearance is immediately its disappearance. We might recall at this point Hegel's admirable pages on the empty tomb and the vain quest of the crusades. Therefore a scission appears here that engenders an

---

[23] Ibid., 122 (trans. altered). – Ricoeur's note.

unending mediation of immediacy. This is why testimony itself first requires interpretation.

Interpretation is required a second time by the critical activity that testimony gives rise to. Testimony may be true or false. It needs therefore to be tested. This tight bond between testimony and a process of examination is not abolished when testimony is transferred from a law court to the plane of reflection. On the contrary, the judicial dimension of testimony then takes on its full depth. "We must always decide between the false witness and the truthful one....[For there is] no manifestation of the absolute without the threat of a false testimony, and without the decision that separates the sign from the idol."[24] This role for judgment will find its counterpart in a moment in the movement by means of which reflection replies to testimony's critique, what Nabert calls the criteriology of the divine.

Lastly, testimony calls for interpretation through a still more fundamental dialectic, the dialectic of the witness and the things seen. On the one hand, to be a witness is to have participated in what one has seen and to be able to testify to it. On the other, testimony may break away from the things seen to such a degree that it gets concentrated on the quality of an act, a work, or a life, which is in itself a sign of the absolute. In this second sense, which is complementary to the first sense, to be a witness is no longer to testify that..., but to testify to.... This latter expression allows us to understand that a witness may so implicate himself in his testimony that it becomes the best test of his conviction. When this test becomes the price of life itself, the witness changes names. He becomes a martyr. In Greek, though, μάρυς [*martus*] means witness. I am well aware that any argument from martyrdom is suspect. A cause that has martyrs is not necessarily a just cause. But martyrdom, precisely, is not an argument and still less a proof. It is a test, a limit situation. A person becomes a martyr because first of all he is a witness.

This proximity between a witness and a martyr nevertheless does have an effect on the very meaning of testimony. Its purely juridical sense totters. In a trial, for example, a witness enjoys immunity. Only the accused risks his life. But a witness can become the accused and the righteous may die. Then a great

[24] Ibid., 146 (trans. altered). – Ricoeur's note.

historical archetype arises: the suffering servant, the persecuted righteous person, Socrates, Jesus....The commitment, the risk assumed by the witness makes testimony more than and other than a simple narration of what was seen. Testimony is also the commitment of a pure heart and a commitment unto death. It thus belongs to the tragic destiny of truth.

This tragic destiny of truth outside of us in a wholly contingent history may accompany the letting go by means of which reflection abandons the illusions of a sovereign consciousness. It does so by internalizing the dialectic of testimony through which it records the trace of the absolute in the contingency of history. The three dialectical moments of testimony – event and meaning, the trial of false testimony, and testimony *about* what is seen and *of* a life – find their echo, their reverberation, in the movement of consciousness that renounces its sovereignty.

The dialectic of event and meaning? A whole structure of self-understanding is declared here that enjoins us to renounce any idea of a self-constituting of consciousness within a purely immanent temporality. We exist because we are seized by those events that *happen* to us in the strong sense of this word – those entirely fortuitous encounters, dramas, moments of happiness or misfortune that, as one says, have completely changed the course of our existence. The task of understanding ourselves through them is the task of transforming the accidental into our destiny. The event is our master. Each of our separate existences are like those communities we belong to – we are absolutely dependent on certain founding events. They are not events that pass away, but events that endure. In themselves, they are event-signs. To understand ourselves is to continue to bear witness and to testify to them.

The dialectic of true and false testimony? This process has its counterpart on the side of reflection in what Nabert calls the criteriology of the divine, and which he couples precisely to the examination of testimony. For a *finite* existence like ours, appropriation can only be a *critical* act. There is no unitary intuition or a form of absolute knowledge in which consciousness would become aware of the absolute and of itself. It is in sorting among and sifting its *predicates* that we seem most likely to signify the divine, that we form a certain idea of it. This sorting takes the form of a trial. It is easy to see why. To discern the predicates of the divine is to follow what medieval thinkers called the way of eminence. For how else are we to carry a certain idea of justice or goodness to extremes if not by conforming our judgment of eminence to the testimony given outside of us in history by the words, the deeds, and the lives of certain exceptional people, who are not necessarily famous, but who testify by their excellence to that very way of eminence that reflection attempts to reproduce in itself and for itself? It appears therefore that the two trials or judgments crisscross: in forming predicates of the divine we disqualify the false witness; in recognizing the true witnesses we identify the predicates of the divine. This fine hermeneutic circle is the law of self-understanding.

But the third dialectic, the dialectic of historical testimony, is the most significant for a self-understanding that would attempt to reproduce its movement in itself. The witness to things seen, we said, at the limit becomes a martyr for truth. Here reflection must confess its inequality with the *historical paradigm* of its movement of letting go, if it is not to abuse its words and become radically deceitful. We use big words: epoché, reflective distance, letting go. But in our use of them we indicate more that we can conceptualize the direction of a movement, that movement we have simply wanted to "point to" with the expression "letting go" as the abandonment of the sovereign consciousness. Philosophy has to internalize what is said in the Gospel: "Who would save his life must lose it." Transposed into the realm of reflection, this means, "Whoever would posit himself as a constituting consciousness will miss his destiny." But reflection cannot produce this renouncing of the sovereign consciousness out of itself without contradicting itself. It can only do so by confessing its total dependence on the historical manifestations of the divine. Nabert expresses this dependence in terms of a complementarity. "For the apprehension of the divine," he says in *Le Désire de Dieu*, "the letting go essential to mystical experience and the connection of the divine to a historical manifestation are complementary to each other. Thanks to the former, the grasping of the divine tends to be confused with the advance of reflection solely through the asceticism of the philosophical consciousness; through the latter, the divine is inscribed in history through a testimony whose meaning consciousness has never exhausted."[25] And a few pages

---

[25] Nabert, *Le Désir de Dieu*, 267. – Ricoeur's note.

later he adds, "The essential idea is to demonstrate a well-founded correspondence between the historical affirmation of the absolute and the degrees through which a consciousness is raised up and transformed by an originary affirmation...."[26] For my part, I would emphasize the non-reciprocal nature of this complementarity inasmuch as the initiative belongs to historical testimony.

To account for this priority of historical testimony over self-consciousness, I would refer you to the description Kant gives of "aesthetic ideas" in the *Critique of Judgment*.[27] You will recall the circumstances in which he makes recourse to this theme. At the moment of accounting for the aesthetic productions of genius, he invokes that power of the imagination "to present" (*Darstellung*) ideas of reason for which we have no concept. By means of such representation, the imagination "occasions much thought [*viel zu denken*], without however any definite thought, i.e., any *concept* being capable of being adequate to it; it consequently cannot be completely compassed and made intelligible by language."[28] Hence what the imagination thus confers on thought is the ability to *think further*.[29]

Historical testimony has the same structure and the same function. It, too, is a "presentation," an "exhibition" [*Darstellung*] of what for reflection remains an idea; namely, the idea of a letting go wherein we affirm an order exempt from that servitude from which finite existence cannot deliver itself. The Kantian relation between an Idea and its aesthetic "presentation" well expresses the kind of relation we are seeking to formulate between originary affirmation – which would require an impossible *total mediation* between self-consciousness and its symbolic experience – and its

---

[26] Ibid., 279. – Ricoeur's note.
[27] Immanuel Kant, *Critique of Judgment*, trans. J. H. Bernard (New York and London: Hafner, 1968), §49. – Ricoeur's note.
[28] Ibid., 157. – Ricoeur's note.
[29] "If we now place under a concept a representation of the imagination belonging to its presentation, but which occasions in itself more thought than can ever be comprehended in a definite concept and which consequently aesthetically enlarges the concept itself in an unbounded fashion, the imagination is here creative, and it brings the faculty of intellectual ideas (the reason) into movement; i.e. by a representation, more thought (which indeed belongs to the concept of the object) is occasioned than can in it be grasped or made clear" (ibid., 158). – Ricoeur's note.

historical presentation in testimonies whose meaning we have never exhausted.

Such is the non-heteronomous dependence of conscious reflection on external testimonies. And it is this dependence that gives philosophy a certain idea of revelation. As earlier with regard to poetic discourse, on the "objective" side of the idea of revelation, so too on the "subjective" side, the experience of testimony can provide no more than the horizon for a specifically religious and biblical experience of revelation, without our ever being able to derive that experience from the purely philosophical categories of truth as manifestation and reflection as testimony.

Allow me to conclude with this expression of a dependence without heteronomy. Why, I will ask at the end of this meditation, is it so difficult for us to conceive of a dependence without heteronomy? Is it not because we too often and too quickly think of a will that submits and not enough of an imagination that opens itself? Beginning from this question it is possible to catch sight of the dividing line between the two sides of our investigation. For what are the poem of the Exodus and the poem of the resurrection, called to mind in the first section, addressed to, if not to our imagination rather than our obedience? And what is the historical testimony that our reflection would like to internalize addressed to, if not to our imagination? If to understand oneself is to understand oneself in front of the text, must we not say that the reader's understanding is suspended, derealized, made potential just as the world itself is metamorphosized by the poem? If this is true, we must say that the imagination is that part of ourselves that responds to the text as a Poem, and that alone can encounter revelation no longer as an unacceptable pretension, but a non-constraining appeal.

5

Salvation Myths and
Contemporary Reason

Let us consider how myths of salvation stand in relation to contemporary ideas of reason.[1] However, before proposing a few themes for discussion directly related to this topic, I want to propose two preliminary analyses that seem to me appropriate for an introductory lecture. I propose first to examine the pertinence of the concept of "salvation myths" in relation to a precise definition of "myth." This will be the object of my opening remarks. Next I shall move on to the concept of a "history of salvation," forged from the exegesis of the Jewish and Christian Bible, which in our cultural tradition helps to make more specific the broader notion of "salvation myths," and which is what really will be at stake in my discussion in the second part of this lecture.

---

[1] Previously unpublished in either French or English, this essay was first published in an Italian translation: "Miti della salvezza e ragione contemporanea," in G. Ferretti, ed., *La ragione e i simboli della salvezza oggi*, atti del quarto colloquio su filosofia e religione (Macerata, 1988), Pubblicazioni della Facoltà di lettere e filosofia, 53 (Marietti, 1990), 15–31.

The Pertinence of the Expression "Salvation Myths"

The background question for our discussions in this meeting seems to me to be whether we can come to some agreement regarding the correct use of the terms "myth" and "salvation."

With Mircea Eliade, I shall speak of myth as a *narrative of origins*. Through its *form*, a myth is a species of the narrative genus. What this formal point of view makes specific is the generally anonymous character of myth, the fact that it cannot be assigned to a particular author. Received from tradition, myths are taken to be worthy of faith by the members of some group, with no other guarantee of their authenticity than the belief of those who transmit them. Through its *content*, a myth is a story about founding events. This is what is meant by speaking of myths as narratives that tell about origins. *Origin* here has to be taken in a broad sense: the origin of the gods, of the world, of human beings, of an institution; the founding of a dynasty, a city, an empire; the introduction of some practice (a ritual, craft, language, writing, and so on). The myth answers the question of the absolute beginning of something that is important to the contemporary human condition in some particular cultural setting. But this beginning – this is the essential point – and the founding events connected with it are situated in an original time, a time that cannot be coordinated with the time of those events historians recount or even with the time of the events story tellers recount. It is this twofold status of myth that I want to hold on to: that it is a narrative about origins, which, on the one hand, takes the form of a traditional story, and, on the other, that this story unfolds on another level than the time of history or of ordinary tales: *in illo tempore* [in *that* time].

If we accept this quite general definition of myth, in what sense may we speak of salvation myths? In our culture shaped by Judeo-Christianity,

> the idea of salvation (gr. *sôzo* and derivatives) is expressed in Hebrew [first] by a group of roots that all relate to the same fundamental experience: to be saved, that is, to be pulled from some danger where one risks perishing. Depending on the nature of the peril, the saving act is akin to protection, liberation, redemption, healing; and salvation to victory, life, peace.... It is starting from

such human experience, and in making use of the same terms that express it, that revelation makes explicit one of the most essential aspects of God's action in the world: God saves human beings, Christ is our savior (Luke 2:11), the Gospel brings salvation to all who believe. (Romans 1:16)[2]

I take this definition from the *Vocabulaire de théologie biblique*, edited by Xavier Léon-Dufour. My next question then is as follows: to what degree do the *narratives* in which "God's action in the world" finds expression stem from the category of "myth"? In my opinion, they do so only at the price of several corrections that will progressively render this category inapplicable and that, within the Judeo-Christian world, at least, require the more specific category of a history of salvation which I shall be taking up in the second part of my remarks.

The category of myth is nevertheless useful as a starting point for situating the specifically Jewish, then Christian notion into a broader *comparative* context. As I did in my earlier work, *The Symbolism of Evil*, I consider this broader background to be the Assyrian-Babylonian world with which Hebrew thought was later to enter into debate, along with those Orphic and tragic parallels to be found in the Greek world into which one day Judaism and Christianity were to inscribe themselves.[3] (I shall say nothing about the Orient or Extreme Orient, about India and China, nor about allegedly "primitive" traditions; I confine myself strictly to what more immediately belongs to our cultural memory.)

It is in connection with the problem of *evil* that the narratives dealing with salvation belong to the world of myths. For, the problem of evil does pose a question relating to its *origin* and, in this sense, does relate to a segment of the narratives that deal with origins, the anthropological segment of a broader cosmogenesis. The question of the origin of evil here is presented as follows: *how* did the human condition with its woes and misfortunes that we deplore through lamentation begin? *Why* suffering and death, hate and murder, the painful character of work and birth – in

---

[2] Xavier Léon-Dufour, ed., *Vocabulaire de théologie biblique* (Paris: Cerf, 1970, 1995), col. 1185.
[3] Paul Ricoeur, *The Symbolism of Evil*, trans. Emerson Buchanan (New York: Harper and Row, 1967).

short, why the "harshness of existence"? Here is where a typology of myths about the origin of evil legitimately can be inscribed in the larger space of myths. This is how, in *The Symbolism of Evil*, I considered four great types of myth relative to the woeful state of our human condition: the theogonic myth – where evil is implied in the originally conflictual structure of the divine; anthopogenesis here is just one episode in the theogony; the orphic myth – which relates evil to the fall of the soul into inferior matter; the tragic myth – which sees misfortune as arising from a *hubris* [or lack of measure] mysteriously connected to the greatest, the best agents, and to the deceitful seduction of a malicious divinity; and finally the Adamic myth – which tells how in an instant, the human beings created good by a good God deviated from their innocent condition following the seduction offered by a perverse entity. Even if we do not confuse the biblical narrative with what deserves to be called a myth of deviance, separation, going astray, rather than one of a fall in the orphic (and Platonic) sense, the narrative found in Genesis does deserve to be called a myth inasmuch as it satisfies our twofold criterion: it is a traditional story relating events situated in a time that cannot be coordinated with the time of human history, which, in the Hebrew Bible, really only begins with the call of Abraham (Genesis 12).

Therefore it is by way of myths that relate to the origin of evil that salvation myths can be considered as myths. They stand in a relationship of *correlation* to myths about the origin of evil that makes them a response to our woeful human condition. There is salvation, therefore, according to our proposed definition, there where something essential to the human condition is threatened, or even already lost. And what is threatened, lost, is precisely a certain integrity in relation to which our woeful condition is experienced and interpreted as being in default. Every origin myth having to do with evil depicts this woeful condition as a loss. Salvation myths, in turn, proclaim something like a reparation, a reintegration, a restoration, which, as I shall say in the second part of my presentation, can be expected to be superior to the lost integrity. In this way, it is possible to make the typology of myths about evil just referred to correspond to a typology of salvation myths. In a mythology that integrates the origin of evil into a cosmogony or a theogony, there is no problematic concerning a salvation distinct from creation. There is properly speaking no room to speak of a history of salvation (an expression I shall return to in a moment). Every drama, every historical struggle has to be tied to the drama of creation through some kind of *repetition*, which takes the form of a "cultic ritual." With the tragic myth, deliverance can be nothing other than the tragic vision itself, placed under the sign of the pair *Phobos* and *Éléos* (terror and pity). There is no history of salvation, in this sense, but rather sympathy, which makes one *participate* in the hero's misfortunes; a kind of weeping-along-with, and the purification of these very tears through the beauty of the tragic verse. Salvation, in this case, is just this purification of the emotions of terror and pity: "suffering in order to understand." This sums up tragic wisdom (*Agamemnon*). As for the orphic myth of the exiled soul, it is perhaps the least "historical" of all. History is the sojourn of the captive soul; the major mode of deliverance is a *purification through knowledge*, through *gnosis*. The movement of withdrawal, evasion, and elevation points to the Platonic reminiscence which is itself a leap outside history.

It is with the Adamic myth that the response of deliverance takes on features that place in question the very pertinence of the concept of a salvation myth. This starts with the narrative of an original fault. The gap that is constitutive of evil is plainly distinguished, within the origin myth, from the first foundation, from the creation which God even declares to be "good, very good" (Genesis 1:31), according to the redactor of the creation story. A history distinct from this immemorial creation is launched. This "historical" aspect is accentuated by the salvation myth as myth. It is by recounting stories that, to be sure, do not satisfy the rational criteria of historiography (which I shall speak about in part three), that the biblical writers speak of the *progress* of salvation. For example, the figure of Abraham is presented as a first response, in human time, to the immemorial figure of Adam. Yes, Abraham is largely a legendary figure, but precisely legend, *saga*, or however one chooses to put it, is a narrative genre distinct from myth, in the strict sense of narratives that deal with origins *in illo tempore*. Legend has to do with very old times which in a way serve as a transition between the time of origins and the chronological time that is common to both the narrator and the things spoken of. Then, as the story unfolds, it is within the very tissue of the history of a people that salvation occurs, from the

Exodus to the settlement in Canaan, then to the time of the monarchy of David and Solomon, where the narrative is close to the historiographical style we find in Herodotus. The myth, if we can still speak of myth, is a myth of history and in history.

A second divergence from mythic temporality is proposed with the articulation, so typical of the biblical world, of traditions and prophecy. Here the literary genre is wholly different from not only origin narratives, but from all those narratives of every kind that bring together, that constitute what Gerhard von Rad has placed under the rubric of a theology of traditions.[4] Prophecy, as a prophecy of misfortune, deflates the confidence placed in the founding tradition that gives narrative identity to Israel; then, as a prophecy of deliverance, it announces a renewal that will be something new; the future will be New. It is this breakthrough toward a future higher than the lost integrity that marks the most significant limit to the idea of a salvation myth. Can we still call this reversal from past to future, toward a non-repetitive future myth?

If there is, nevertheless, one domain where the notion of a salvation myth retains its pertinence, it is with the *apocalyptic* mode that has produced myths of the End symmetrical to the myths of the Origin. There is a continuity of meaning here that links together prophecy, eschatology, and apocalyptic. Prophecy stands in relation to historical time as turned toward *imminent* events coming from an impending future. In turn, this sense of imminence projects a horizon of hope that merits the name eschatology, inasmuch as it implies something like an end of history, a denouement that will be a deliverance, hence salvation. But so long as eschatology remains in solidarity with prophecy, it does not break the connection between the end and the course of history. To this eschatology belong the figures of the Anointed, the Messiah and, equally – albeit in a different sense, which I shall return to in part two – the figure of the Suffering Servant, the *Erbed Yahweh* of Second Isaiah (Isaiah 40–55). Apocalyptic represents another nature than does this eschatology connected with prophecy. In the technical sense of the term, Apocalypses (which are innumerable, the canon of the Hebrew scriptures having only

[4] Gerhard von Rad, *Old Testament Theology*, 2 vols, trans. D. M. G. Stalker (New York: Harper, 1962–5).

retained that of the book of Daniel, and the Christian canon that of John) describe special revelations made to an initiate, often assimilated to an archaic figure, to whom are unveiled secrets relating to the "last things," the torments of the "last days," in short, to the "End" of history. But this End is wholly heterogeneous to the time of history. For this reason, the eschatological symbolism of apocalypses does merit being compared to that of myth, for it is no longer a question of an Origin, but of the End. The response to the *Urzeit* [Primal Time] is to be found in an *Endzeit* [End Time]. This reversal of the canonic signification of the term *myth*, from origin to end, is legitimated by the symmetry between the two temporal positions of the Beginning and the End, neither of which can be coordinated with historical time. The coming Kingdom is to hope what immemorial Creation is to the memory of the most distant past, with eschatology serving as the transition between history and its end, just as legend served as a transition between history and its beginning.

The History of Salvation and the Myth of Salvation

It is the supra-historical dimension of myth that we next need to confront with the intra-historical dimension of what many exegetes and theologians have called a "history of salvation," as a translation of the German *Heilsgeschichte*. This expression designates the theological motif that unifies, only to a certain point, the narrative texts of the Hebrew and Christian Bible, as we shall see at the end of this section. To put it in a few words, this theological motif signifies that God is the master of history, that God guides it toward fulfillment, but in and through history, that is, with the help of human agents. We need to acknowledge that this motif, which we can see enters into competition with other such motifs, is never elaborated at the systematic level I am using to state it, but rather with the narrative resources of biblical discourse.

It is these resources that we next need to list and explore.

(a) The first feature I would like to emphasize has to do with the *typological* connection that gives a specific style to the biblical narratives. Underlying the mere succession in the narratives a~ complex *correspondences* that bring together the origin narra~

of a quite different structure. The most noteworthy of these is the correspondence between Promise and Fulfillment, which finds an anchorage in the Hebraic notion of the Covenant. More exactly speaking, this correspondence plays out between a series of covenants – with Noah, with Abraham, with David, and so on – which do not simply succeed one another but in a way build on one another. Biblical time, in this sense, is a cumulative time within which these Covenants mutually reinforce one another. I must say here that I was impressed and seduced regarding this point by Northrop Frye's typological exegesis in his *The Great Code*.[5] Armed with experience refined through his work on literary criticism, Frye delights in reconstituting the rhythm of alternating ascending and descending movements, with their highs and lows. Between these high points and low points Frye draws two interweaving lines of correspondence that make them the "type" or "anti-type" of each other. The table of these correspondences is precisely what makes up William Blake called the "Great Code." Three components of a *Heilsgeschichte* can be drawn from this reconstruction: a relation between promise and fulfillment, a cumulative character of history, and the counterpoint of a twofold typology. In these three different forms the *correspondence* relation assures a unity to a unique genre that requires a concept distinct from that of a salvation myth. In truth, the *Heilsgeschichte* is a myth of salvation only to the degree that the typological correspondence remains subordinated to the polarity of an *Urzeit* and an *Endzeit*. This is especially true if we confine ourselves to listing the canonical organization of the texts that makes Genesis and Revelation the framework that frames the history between them. But as we shall see, there are other resources that make the in-betweenness of history acquire its own consistency, which removes it from the tutelage of these two mythical poles.

(b) The second feature of a *Heilsgeschichte* I want now to consider is quite close to the preceding one and does not yet call in question the exclusive reading of a theology of salvation in terms of a *Heilsgeschichte*. I have already mentioned that this concept was forged by exegetical theologians concerned to find

Frye, *The Great Code* (London: Routledge and Kegan Paul, ~k: Harcourt Brace Jovanovich; 1983).

an order, a dominant theme in the Scriptures, particularly the Hebrew Bible. The success of this interpretation until recently rests in large part on the fact that the final order retained through the closing of the canon gives the appearance of one *grand narrative*, superimposed on multiple and divergent traditions. This redactional work began with the so-called "Jahwehist" school to which we owe the principal core of the Pentateuch (the five "Books of Moses"). It consists in particular in aligning along a single temporal axis heterogeneous narratives, myths, legends, short stories (the story of David, for example), accounts close to historiography (the ascension of David, the succession to David's throne), in such a way that they unfold like a single plot running from the Creation to the end of the monarchy. The successors to the "Jahwist" extend this narrative space to include the return from exile and the restoration of what is called the Second Temple. What is important for my thesis is not so much the holding onto the origin myths as their narrativization through entering into the gravitational field of the great narrative centered on the election of Israel. This way of setting side by side the myth of Creation, the call of Abraham, the legends of the Patriarchs, the deliverance from Egypt, the revelation at Sinai, the conquest and settlement in Canaan, and so on, creates the appearance of a single story-line unfolding in homogeneous time. The resulting alignment reflects a consummate art of narration. We understand its meaning even better when we connect it to the function exercised by this grand narrative, namely, assuring the narrative identity of a people by unifying its traditions into one grand narrative. In this sense, this grand narrative is constitutive of the self-understanding of the people of Israel. Undoubtedly, it was in this way that the Hebrews most distinguished themselves from the Greeks, who chose instead a cosmological and political understanding of their identity.

It is on the basis of the model offered by this narrative, which we may speak of as confessional, that the primitive Christian Church understood how its founder was inscribed in history. His coming was seen both as the fulfillment of the Scriptures, hence of the prior grand narrative, and as opening an intermediary time between the Resurrection and the Parousia. Luke the Gospel writer is the architect in this regard of an extending of the grand narrative, whereby the Acts of the Apostles trace the initial lines of this history of "between times." The delay of the Parousia will constitute the first major crisis for this theology of history and lead to having to take universal history into account and to articulating this as the history of a new "People of God." This immense work of thought will find a provisional point of equilibrium in the vision of history recorded by Saint Augustine in his *The City of God*.[6] This in turn will be just one link in a long series of theologies of history that runs from the Jahwist to... Hegel!

(c) I would like now to submit to critical reflection the ambition of those exegetes and theologians who thought they could identify the biblical notion of salvation with a *Heilsgeschichte*. It was principally against the narrative expression of this *Heilsgeschichte* in a rectilinear "grand narrative" unfolding in a homogeneous time that exegesis more attentive to the variety and diversity of the canonical writings of the Bible was directed. The deliverance from evil which makes up salvation is spoken of not just through narrative. Alongside the narratives there are laws, prophecies, wisdom writings, and hymns wherein praise and lamentation both occur. A multiple naming of God results from this polyphony, this plurality of voices. It is one thing to speak *of* God as the supreme actor of some collective tale, another to speak *in the name of* God as the legislator or prophet, to speak *to* God as in the chanting of the Psalms, or to speak *about* God like the sage. This multiple naming of God corresponds to a multiple approach to salvation. For example, the faithful obedience to the commandments has the value of liberation, in the sense of a returning to true life; and following the path of justice is another way of being saved. For the prophets of promise, salvation inseparably signifies both historical deliverance and the establishing of justice. "Justice and salvation," this composite expression tends to become a technical expression for the promise. As for the lamentations uttered by the suppliants of the Psalms, they echo with perils of every kind. God is salvation as the recourse of the just, the poor, the persecuted, those of pure heart, and those whose spirits have been laid low. Their prayer ends in a cry: "Save us, Jahweh!" To be sure, an overall historical perspective is never completely absent from the praise of the suppliant who has been

[6] Saint Augustine, *The City of God Against the Pagans*, trans. R. W Dyson (Cambridge: Cambridge University Press, 1998).

answered, and consolation remains closely tied to the expectation of a final reign of justice. But through such texts the idea of salvation frees up a whole range of harmonics capable of multiple developments. In this respect, the imposition of the form of one grand narrative on the diversity of texts and literary genres risks doing violence to the pluralistic richness of the theme of salvation.

A second critique addressed to the content of the very idea of salvation can be added to this first critique drawn from the diversity of literary genres and particularly from the diversity of types of narrative leveled down by the grand narrative. In its most rudimentary form, this idea coincides with the election of Israel among the nations and finds its most militant expression in the theme of the "wars of Jahweh." Yet the test of exile, without really weakening the theme of election, renders it solidary with the experience of misfortune. As André Néher puts it, in *L'Essence du prophétisme*, a "slice of nihilation" gets integrated into the life of a people who henceforth will think of themselves as survivors.[7] Even more so, today, after Auschwitz.... Next, to this idea of a historical salvation passing through extreme misfortune had to be joined the idea of an advance of salvation by way of an enemy: "Cyrus is my servant," says God.[8] Henceforth it will be through the mediation of divine rule over the nations that the salvation of Israel will be realized. At the same time, the ways of the Lord appear to be unfathomable and more and more difficult to decipher from the course of events. But there is something still more grave: a certain coherence of history will remain associated with what ever since Hegel we call a "moral vision of the world." It was for its sins that Israel was punished. In this way, the theology of history makes itself tributary to a theory of *retribution*. It is this theodicy before the letter that some of the wisdom writings, particularly Job, call into question. The scandal and enigma of *unjust suffering* displaces attention from the global destiny of a

[7] Néher actually says "a slice of non-history," and speaks of a "negation of history," and of a "mystery of negation," which introduces a new history. André Néher, *L'Essence du prophétisme* (Paris: Presses Universitaires de France, 1955); reprinted as *Prophètes et prophéties: L'Essence du prophétisme* (Paris: Payot, 2004), 203–4.

[8] Isaiah 44:28.

people or peoples toward the unmerited misfortune of individuals, for which no theodicy can answer. However we may interpret the closing verses of Job, the flash of lightning conveyed by the end of this book seems unrelated – explicitly or even implicitly – to a profession of faith relating to the end of history. We are far from a *Heilsgeschichte* centered on the election of Israel.

I want to end this review of resistances to the schema of a *Heilsgeschichte*, within the Scriptures themselves, with a more personal reflection on the place of the Christ symbol in the "grand narrative." As a first approximation, its place is indicated as a zero time – Dumezil would call it an *axial* time – separating before and after; the before of all the events that the Old Testament had already given linear form from Creation to the end of prophecy, the after as announced by the Acts of the Apostles and projected as leading to a Last Judgment. Here we have a vast extrapolation of the theology of history implicit in the J document, supported by the correspondences and typological relations internal to the Old Testament I have spoken of. Furthermore, the apocalyptic vision of the last days finds more than an illustration and already a realization in Jesus' preaching of the Kingdom of God. In this way, the Christ event reorients the grand narrative by giving it a new center. (Among modern exegetes, Oscar Cullman is the one who has most contributed to accrediting this linear version of the Christian *Heilsgeschichte* in his *Christ and Time*.)[9] But if the Christ *event* allows itself to be integrated into this grand narrative, the *symbol* indissociably attached to it tends, in my opinion, to shatter this grand narrative. I find indications of this possible critique of this schema even within the New Testament in Saint Paul. In I Corinthians 1:17–37, he proclaims the "Logos of the Cross" as folly: "But God chose what is foolish in the world to shame the wise; God chose what is weak in the world to shame the strong; God chose what is low and despised in the world, things that are not, to reduce to nothing things that are, so that one might boast in the presence of God" (1:27–9). And in the admirable hymn of Philippians 2:5–11, the Christ is he who, although "having the form of God," "*emptied* himself, taking the form of a slave" and "humbled himself and became obedient to

[9] Oscar Cullman, *Christ and Time: The Primitive Christian Conception of Time and History*, trans. Floyd Filson (London: SCM, 1962).

the point of death." Twice *nothing*, the nothingness of the Kenosis after the nothingness of foolishness, is designated as the point of passage toward the "power" in 1 Corinthians and "exaltation" in Philippians. The connection to a theology of history is certainly not broken (Romans 11 outlines a similar schema where Jews and pagans receive a definite destiny), but if not broken, it can no longer take the form of an immediately readable and decipherable march toward triumph and glory. No royal way passes through "foolishness" and "kenosis." We can still speak of "power," but only in and through weakness. In this regard, a political reading of religion like that Marcel Gauchet proposes in *The Disenchantment of the World* is highly instructive, even if it does not exhaust the meaning of religion.[10] It is legitimated by the *Heilsgeschichte* inasmuch as it associates salvation with the triumph in which the elect participate. But the theme of the Kingdom of God cannot be divested of its political resonance. With Jesus, Gauchet emphasizes, the logic of domination of the apocalyptic writers is overturned. Jesus, he says, is a "diametrical inverted Messiah": "While the monarch of the world was *at the top* of the human pyramid, Jesus was *at the bottom*, just like any other ordinary human.... He was the perfect *counterpart* to the imperial mediator, one *at the opposite pole*."[11] My question then is as follows: At what price does this reversal of the figure of a powerful messiah allow itself to be inscribed in a grand narrative that runs from Genesis to the Book of Revelation? One thing is certain. The axial moment represented by the Christ *event*, in Jesus of Nazareth, signifies at the same time, on a *symbolic* level, kenosis of the principle. We cannot fail to regroup the negative figures encountered on our way around this "nothing" of foolishness and kenosis: the "slice of nihilation" by which Néher characterizes the Jewish exile, the suffering servant from Second Isaiah, Job's revolt. We ought not to say that the Resurrection wipes all this away. It "took place so as to confirm the exemplary necessity of passing through extreme abandonment and humiliation."[12] The only way to give

---

[10] Marcel Gauchet, *The Disenchantment of the World: A Political History of Religion*, trans. Oscar Burge (Princeton: Princeton University Press, 1997).

[11] Ibid., 119.

[12] Ibid., 121.

the Passion a historical continuation would be to make the Cross the guideline of a history centered on victims and not on conquerors. And this new paradigm cannot fail to unravel the grand narrative inasmuch as this latter tends to be confused with a history of domination and a ground for domination. But we *do not know* – in the strong sense of the word *know* – how a history of victims can be inscribed in a meta-history that ends well. We do not know, not only because we have no dialectic, which like Hegel's cunning of reason will make misfortune end in the triumph of the Spirit, but also because the history of suffering itself does not form a system (like, in *The City of God*, profane history finds itself intermingled with sacred history). Only a history of domination, it seems, forms a system. Perhaps the secret kinship among all kinds of suffering – between the Passion and Auschwitz – defies every one of our rational conceptions of negativity and of the negation of negation. The history of victimization or rather the histories of victims do not tolerate being included in the continual history of domination, like some surpassed – *aufgehoben* – moment, nor do they line up with that history as another coherent history. Evil is Legion (Mark 5:9). Which is why its appearances challenge every grand narrative.

If therefore the tie between foolishness and kenosis, on the one hand, and power and exaltation, on the other, cannot be known through a rational account, and even cannot be recounted, inscribed in some grand narrative, it must be the object of a hope that respects the mystery.

The Myth of Salvation and Contemporary Reason

As I stated in my opening remarks, I am limiting myself to setting out some themes for discussion during our conference.

(a) First of all, I propose that we limit ourselves to the conflict between *mythos* and *logos* on the plane of history, inasmuch as the idea of salvation, within the Judeo-Christian world, has to a greater or lesser extent been identified with that of a *Heilsgeschichte* and where this gets expressed on the literary level in terms of a grand narrative running from Genesis to the Apocalypse. I do not believe it is necessary to deplore this limit which, in fact, leaves a vast field open to discussion. As a history of beginnings, myth joins human destiny to that of the Cosmos. And within the domain of the Jewish and Christian Scriptures, the theology of history has considerable implications that extend as far as physics and astronomy. The debates arising from a literal reading of Genesis, from Galileo to Darwin, bear witness to this. We need only to think of the furious battles arising from the allegation that the world is 6,000 years old, which a venerable tradition adds to such a literal reading of Genesis. In this regard, we ought not to underestimate the amount of damage caused by a misunderstanding of the specificity of mythic language, a misunderstanding encouraged by aligning heterogeneous time spans within one grand narrative. How many battles have been fought in vain and finally lost by different forms of Jewish and Christian orthodoxy on the fronts of astronomy, geology (that over fossils!), biology (that over evolution!), and anthropology (that over prehumans!). On all these fronts, reason remains the victor. The benefit for faith is to have reached a deeper and truer understanding of myth as language that deals with foundations, on another plane than that of scientific knowledge.

(b) If then we remain within the field of the philosophy and the theology of history, in the sense that history is that of human beings in their life circumstances, it seems to me that an important line for discussion has to do with the *epistemology* of history, understood as historiography that has a scientific vocation. Between myth and history, the opposition seems to be total, as a first approximation.

At the level of contents, we have the very notion of a narrative in which the origins unfold in an original time distinct from that of everyday reality. Yet this latter wants only to acknowledge events that can be inscribed in a calendar time, itself based on astronomical science.

At the level of form, the notion of a *traditional* narrative, drawing its authority from its mode of transmission, is rejected by historiography that seeks proof in documents, that is, in the conserved traces of the narrated events. Documentary proof in this regard constitutes the "epistemological break" that separates historiography from myth, legend, stories, epics, and finally from every fictional narrative.

In my opinion, the birth of historiography calls for an investigation into the functions of myth that do not allow its being reduced to an explanation of a historical type. But it would be necessary first to have laid out as different language games all the species of narrative, as I did in distinguishing myth, legend, story, chronicle. On the basis of such a typology of narrative forms, a discussion between the phenomenology of myth and that of historiography could well prove fruitful. Earlier I referred to one of these functions of myth that cannot be converted into historiography, namely, the foundational function of a narrative identity for a community that both produces and receives these narratives. This function belongs to the self-understanding of such a community. This interpretation is particularly pertinent in the case of Israel and following it, the early Church, which both had an essentially historical understanding of themselves, in a sense of the term history that does not refer to the *knowledge* of events, but to a way of situating themselves within the *course* of events. I said that for Israel the act of recounting immediately has a confessional dimension. Its narrative is a *confessional narration*. It may well be that no people can elaborate its narrative identity without some recourse to such foundational myths. We need only think of the ancient Romans, or the fathers of the American Revolution, or the way the French Republic invokes the French Revolution.

This foundational function cannot continue to be professed unless we have a less naively unilinear conception of time and unless we become aware of heterogeneous character of different time spans. It would be the function of a meditation on the hierarchy of degrees of depth of different time spans to make room for an idea of a foundation in a time qualitatively different from the time unfolded by historical knowledge.

(c) The problem posed by *Heilsgeschichte* as a total vision of history organized in terms of its End is more difficult to deal with. As already stated, salvation myths, to the degree that we still accept this expression, are responses to origin myths. Yet the break that has occurred in our own culture, with myths of the End, came later than that with myths about the Beginning. It is easy to understand why. Action has a greater need of some orientation toward the future than it does a foundation in the past. Before the modern or post-modern crisis over grand narratives, our rational culture went through an age of Enlightenment that secularized its Judeo-Christian *Heilsgeschichte*. Belief in *progress* came to function like a myth of the End, at least until recently.

The question is whether a society can live without a collective project, a directive utopian idea. This is the question Reinhardt Koselleck poses in his *Futures Past*: the structure of historical time, not as represented, but as lived and lived in, constituted by the polarity of a horizon of expectation and a space of experience, can it be surpassed?[13] Can there still be a horizon of expectation when there is no longer any utopia, when we have left behind what Ernst Bloch called the Principle of Hope?[14] Our Western directive utopia was derived from Jewish and Christian hope, structured by the sequence from prophecy to eschatology to apocalyptic, referred to earlier. But the secularized form of *Heilsgeschichte* has been no less submitted to disenchantment than has been its theological archetype. For this reason, a fruitful dialogue between Jewish and Christian hope and the secularized hope stemming from the Enlightenment and taken up by Marxism seems to me to be more than ever necessary. Neither tradition can save us – it has to be said – unless brought together.

(d) A final path for reflection is opened by the internal critique addressed to the grand narrative that gives the *Heilsgeschichte* its narrative form, and by way of that critique, by the insinuated doubt concerning the very pertinence of any *Heilsgeschichte* schema. What has been called into question in this way is the intelligibility of a totalizing process. But the offer, the proclamation of salvation does not take place only through narratives and these themselves cannot be unified into one meaningful grand narrative. Moreover, I ask myself whether the Christ symbol does not introduce a break in principle, thanks to the passage through the nothing that is foolishness and the kenosis. Does not the Christ symbol bring about what Sartre would have called a *detotalization* of every totalization as always premature and misleading? It is principally the "Logos of the Cross" that seems to me to be the core challenge to any triumphal *Heilsgeschichte*. Yet while I raise this question, I also leave it unanswered. Just as the

---

[13] Reinhard Koselleck, *Futures Past: On the Semantics of Historical Time*, trans. Keith Tribe (Cambridge, MA: MIT Press, 1985).

[14] Ernst Bloch, *The Principle of Hope*, 3 vols, trans. Neville Plaice, Stephen Plaice, and Paul Knight (Cambridge, MA: MIT Press, 1986).

idea of progress was for the modern period the secularized equivalent of an assuring *Heilsgeschichte*, do we not see today, in a time some speak of as post-modern, a possible new conversation between the preaching of the folly of the Cross and Christ's Kenosis and the Hegelian philosophy of history? If we then ask what Christians may still specifically have to say, I would answer it is about the hope that, in a way we do not fully understand, the partial histories of victims, histories riddled with defeats, that collaborates with the coming Kingdom of God. Surely, itself a foolish hope...

Works Cited

Adorno, Theodor W. *Aesthetic Theory*, ed. Gretel Adorno and Rolf Tiedemann; trans. Robert Hullot-Kentor. Minneapolis: University of Minnesota Press, 1997.

Albert, Hans. *Treatise on Critical Reason*, trans. Mary Varney Rorty. Princeton: Princeton University Press, 1985.

Apel, Karl-Otto. *From a Transcendental–Semiotic Point of View*, ed. Marianna Papstephanou. Manchester: Manchester University Press, 1998.

———. *Towards a Transformation of Philosophy*, trans. Glyn Adey and David Frisby. London: Routledge and Kegan Paul, 1980.

———. *Transformation der Philosophie*, vol. 1. Frankfurt: Suhrkamp, 1976.

———. *Understanding and Explanation: A Transcendental-Pragmatic Perspective*, trans. Georgia Warnke. Cambridge, MA: MIT Press, 1984.

Augustine. *The City of God Against the Pagans*, trans. R. W Dyson. Cambridge: Cambridge University Press, 1998.

Azouvi, François. *Maine de Biran: La Science de l'homme*. Paris: Vrin, 1995.

———. "Homo Duplex," *Gesnerus* 42 (1985): 229–44.

Baudelaire, Charles. *Les Fleurs du mal*, ed. A. Adam. Paris: Garnier, 1961.

———. *The Flowers of Evil*, trans. Keith Waldrop. Middleton, CT: Wesleyan University Press, 2007.

Beardsley, Monroe. *Aesthetics: Problems in the Philosophy of Criticism*. New York: Harcourt, Brace and World, 1958; Indianapolis: Hackett, 1988.

——. "The Metaphorical Twist," *Philosophy and Phenomenological Research* 22 (1962): 293–307.

Benveniste, Emile. *Problems in General Linguistics*, trans. Mary Elizabeth Meeks. Coral Gables: University of Miami Press, 1971.

Berggren, Douglas. "The Use and Abuse of Metaphor, I and II." *Review of Metaphysics* 16 (1962): 237–58, 450–72.

Biser, Eugen. *Theologische Sprachtheorie und Hermeneutik*. Munich: Kösel, 1970.

Black, Max. *Models and Metaphors*. Ithaca: Cornell University Press, 1962.

Blumenberg, Hans. *Der Prozess der Theoretischen Neugierde*. Frankfurt: Suhkamp, 1973.

Bloch, Ernst. *The Principle of Hope*, 3 vols, trans. Neville Plaice, Stephen Plaice, and Paul Knight. Cambridge, MA: MIT Press, 1986.

Boerhaave, Herman. *Praelectiones academicae de morbis nervorum*. Leyden: Jacob van Eems, 1761.

Bollnow, Otto F. "Zum Begriff der hermeneutischen Logik." In Otto Pöggeler, ed. *Hermeneutische Philosophie: Zehn Aufsätze*. Munich: Nymphenburger, 1972, 100–22.

Bouveresse, Jacques. *La Parole malheureuse: de l'alchimie linguistique à la grammaire philosophique*. Paris: Minuit, 1971.

Brand, Gerd. *Die grundlegenden Texte von Ludwig Wittgenstein*. Frankfurt: Suhrkamp, 1975.

Bubner, Rudiger. "Über die wissenschaftstheoretische Rolle der Hermeneutik," in *Dialektik und Wissenschaft*. Frankfurt: Suhrkamp, 1973, 89–111.

Coleridge, Samuel Taylor. *Biographia Literaria*. The Collected Works, vol. 7, ed. J. Engell and W. Jackson Bate. Princeton: Princeton University Press, 1983. [in two parts]

Coseriu, Eugnio. *Die Geschichte der Sprachphilosophie von der Antik bis zur Gegenwart: Eine Übersicht*, 2 vols. Stuttgart: TBL-Verlag, 1969–72.

Cullman, Oscar. *Christ and Time: The Primitive Christian Conception of Time and History*, trans. Floyd Filson. London: SCM, 1962.

Danto, Arthur. *Analytical Philosophy of History*. New York: Cambridge University Press, 1965.

——. "Basic Actions," *American Philosophical Quarterly* 2 (1965): 141–8.

Dilthey, Wilhem.*Gesammelte Schriften*, vol. 14 (Göttingen: Vandenhoeck and Ruprecht, 1946.

——. *Hermeneutics and the Study of History*, Selected Works, vol. 4, ed. Rudolf A. Makkreel and Frithjof Rodi. Princeton: Princeton University Press, 1996.

———. *Leben Schleiermachers*. Berlin: G. Reimer, 1870.

Donagan, Alan. *The Theory of Morality*. Chicago: University of Chicago Press, 1977.

Dray, William. *Laws and Explanation in History*. New York: Oxford University Press, 1957.

Ebeling, Gerhard. *Word and Faith*, trans. James W. Leitch. Philadelphia: Fortress Press, 1976.

Fahrenbach, Helmut. "Die logisch-hermeneutische Problemstellung in Wittgensteins '*Tractatus*'," *Hermeneutik und Dialektik*, 2: 25–54

———. "Positionen und Probleme gegenwärtigen Philosophie, Teil II: Philosophie der Sprache," *Theologische Rundschau* 35 (1970): 277–306; 36 (1971): 125–44, 221–43.

Fløistad, Guttorm, ed. *Contemporary Philosophy: A New Survey*, vol. 1: *Philosophy of Language*. The Hague: Martinus Nijhoff, 1981.

Foucault, Michel. *The Archaeology of Knowledge*, trans. Alan Sheridan (New York: Pantheon, 1972.

Frey, Daniel. "Entre la méthode et le style: usages de l'herméneutique chez Ricoeur." In C. Sautereau and S. Catonguay, eds, *Usages de l'herméneutique*. Laval: Presses de l'Université de Laval, forthcoming.

Fruchon, Pierre. *Existence humaine et Révélation: Essais d'herméneutique*. Paris: Cerf, 1976.

Gadamer, Hans-Georg. *Truth and Method*, 2nd, rev. edn, rev. and trans. Joel Weinsheimer and Donald G. Marshall. New York: Crossroad, 1991.

———. *Wahrheit und Methode: Grundzüge einer philosophischen Hermeneutik*. Tübingen: Mohr/Siebeck, 1960, 1965, ³1967.

Gadamer, Hans-Georg and Gottfried Boehm, eds. *Seminar: die Hermeneutik und die Wissenschaften*. Frankfurt: Suhrkamp, 1978.

Gauchet, Marcel. *The Disenchantment of the World: A Political History of Religion*, trans. Oscar Burge. Princeton: Princeton University Press, 1997.

Grau, Gerd G., ed. *Probleme der Ethik*. Freiburg: Alber, 1972.

Greimas, A.-J. *Structural Semantics*, trans. Daniele McDowell, Ronald Schleifer, and Alan Velie. Lincoln: University of Nebraska Press, 1983.

Greisch, Jean. *L'Âge herméneutique de la raison*. Paris: Cerf, 1985.

Greisch, Jean and Richard Kearney, eds. *Paul Ricoeur: Les Métamorphoses de la raison herméneutique*. Paris: Cerf, 1991.

Habermas, Jürgen. *Knowledge and Human Interests*, trans. Jeremy J. Shapiro. Boston: Beacon Press, 1971.

———. *On the Logic of the Social Sciences*, trans. Shierry Weber Nicholsen, and Jerry A. Stark. Cambridge, MA: MIT Press, 1988.

———. *Theory and Practice*, trans. John Viertel. Boston: Beacon Press, 1973.

——. *Toward a Rational Society: Student Protest, Science, and Politics,* trans. Jeremy J. Shapiro. Boston: Beacon Press, 1970.

——. "Vorbereitenede Bemerkungen zu einer Theorie der Kommunikativen Kompetenz." In Jürgen Habermas and Nicholas Luhmann, *Theorie der Gesellschaft oder Sozialtechnologie?* (Frankfurt: Suhrkamp, 1971), 101–42.

Hampshire, Stuart. *Thought and Action.* Notre Dame, IN: University of Notre Dame Press, 1983.

Hegel, G. W. F. *Phenomenology of Spirit,* trans. A. V. Miller. New York: Oxford University Press, 1977.

Heidegger, Martin. *Being and Time,* trans. John Macquarrie and Edward Robinson. New York: Harper and Brothers, 1962.

——. *On the Way to Language,* trans. Peter D. Hertz. New York: Harper and Row, 1971.

Heinrichs, Norbert. *Bibliographie der Hermeneutik und ihrer Anwendungsbereiche seit Schleiermacher.* Düsseldorf: Philosophia, 1968.

Hempel, Carl G. "The Function of General Laws in History," *Journal of Philosophy* 39 (1942): 35–48.

Henry, Michel. *The Essence of Manifestation,* trans. Girard Etzkorn. The Hague: Martinus Nijhoff, 1973.

——. *Marx,* 2 vols. Paris: Gallimard, 1976.

——. *Marx: A Philosophy of Human Reality,* trans. Kathleen McLaughlin. Bloomington: Indiana University Press, 1983.

Hirsch, E. D. *Validity in Interpretation.* New Haven: Yale University Press, 1967.

Iser, Wolfgang. *The Act of Reading: A Theory of Aesthetic Response.* Baltimore: Johns Hopkins Univesity Press, 1978.

——. *The Implicit Reader: Patterns of Communication in Prose Literature from Bunyan to Beckett.* Baltimore: Johns Hopkins University Press, 1974.

Janik, Allan and Stephen Toulmin. *Wittgenstein's Vienna.* New York: Simon and Schuster, 1973.

Jauss, Hans Robert. *Kleine Apologie der ästhetischen Erfahrung.* Konstanz: Universitätsverlag, 1972.

——. *Aesthetic Experience and Literary Hermeneutics,* trans. Michael Shaw. Minneapolis: University of Minnesota Press, 1982.

Kant, Immanuel. *Critique of Judgment,* trans. J. H. Bernard. New York and London: Hafner, 1968.

——. *Groundwork for the Metaphysics of Morals,* in *Practical Philosophy,* The Cambridge Edition of the Works of Immanuel Kant, trans. and ed. Mary J. Gregor. Cambridge: Cambridge University Press, 1996.

Kisiel, Theodore. "Zu einer Hermeneutik naturwissenschaftlicher Entdeckung," *Zeitschrift für allgemeine Wissenschaftstheorie* 2 (1971): 195–221.

Klibansky, Raymond, ed. *Contemporary Philosophy: A Survey*. Firenze: La Nuova Italia, 1969.

Kockelmans, Joseph J., ed. *On Heidegger and Language*. Evanston: Northwestern University Press, 1972.

Kossellek, K. R. and W.-D. Stempel, eds. *Poetik und Hermeneutik: Arbeitsergebnisse einer Forschungsgruppe*, 8 vols. Munich: Fink, 1970.

Koselleck, Reinhard. *Futures Past: On the Semantics of Historical Time*, trans. Keith Tribe. Cambridge, MA: MIT Press, 1985.

Levi, Edward H. *An Introduction to Legal Reasoning*. Chicago: University of Chicago Press, 1949.

Levinas, Emmanuel. *Totality and Infinity: An Essay on Exteriority*, trans. Alphonso Lingis. Pittsburgh: Duquesne University Press, 1969.

——. *Otherwise than Being or Beyond Essence*, trans. Alphonso Lingis. Dordrecht: Kluwer, 1991.

Lipps, Hans. *Untersuchungen zu einer hermeneutischen Logik*. Frankfurt: Klostermann, 1938, 1959.

Lorenzmeir, Theodor. *Exegese und Hermeneutik: Eine vergleichende Darstellung der Theologie Rudolf Bulmanns, Herbert Brauns und Gerhard Ebelings*. Hamburg: Furche, 1968.

Loretz, Oswald and Walter Strolz, eds. *Die hermeneutische Frage in der Theologie*. Freiburg: Herder, 1968.

Lotman, Jurij M. *The Structure of the Artistic Text*, Michigan Slavic Contributions, no. 7, trans. Ronald Vroon and Gail Vroon. Ann Arbor: Department of Slavic Languages and Literature, 1977.

Lukács, Georg. *History and Class Consciousness: Studies in Marxist Dialectics*, trans. Rodney Livingstone. Cambridge, MA: MIT Press, 1971.

Macann, Christopher, ed. *Martin Heidegger: Critical Assessments*. London: Routledge and Kegan Paul, 1991.

MacIntyre, Alasdair, *After Virtue: A Study in Moral Theory*. Notre Dame, IN: University of Notre Dame Press, 1981.

Maldiney, Henri. *Aîtres de la langue et demeures de la pensée*. Lausanne: L'Âge d'homme, 1975.

Margolis, Joseph, ed. *Philosophy Looks at the Arts: Contemporary Readings in Aesthetics*. Philadelphia: Temple University Press, 1987.

Melden, A. I. *Free Action*. London: Routledge and Kegan Paul, 1961.

Merleau-Ponty, Maurice. *Phenomenology of Perception*, trans. Colin Smith. London: Routledge and Kegan Paul, 1962.

———. *The Visible and the Invisible*, ed. Claude Lefort, trans. Alphonso Lingis. Evanston: Northwestern University Press, 1968.

Mueller-Vollmer, Kurt, ed., *The Hermeneutic Reader*. Oxford: Blackwell, 1986.

Mukarovsky, J. *Kapitel als der Poetik*. Frankfurt: Suhrkamp, 1970.

Néher, André. *Prophètes et prophétiès: L'Essence du prophetisme*. Paris: Payot, 1955.

Ormiston, Gayle and Alan D. Schrift, eds. *The Hermeneutic Tradition: From Ast to Ricoeur*. Albany: State University of New York Press, 1990.

Palmer, Richard. *Hermeneutics: Interpretation Theory in Schleiermacher, Dilthey, Heidegger, and Gadamer*. Evanston: Northwestern University Press, 1969.

Pannenberg, Wolfhart. "Hermeneutics and Universal History," trans. Paul J. Achtemeier, *Journal for Theology and the Church* 4 (1967): 122–52.

Pareyson, Luigi. *Verità e interpretazionei*. Milan: Mursia, 1971.

Pascal, Blaise. *Pensées*, ed. and trans. by Roger Ariew. Indianapolis: Hackett, 2005.

———. "Prière pour demander à Dieu le bon usage des maladies." In L. Lafuma, ed., *Œuvres complètes*. Paris: Seuil, 1963, 362–5.

Pöggeler, Otto. *Hermeneutische Philosophie: Zehn Aufsätze*. Munich: Nymphenberger, 1972.

———. *Philosophie und Politik bei Heidegger*. Freiburg: Alber, 1972.

———. ed. *Heidegger: Perspektiven zur Deutung seines Werkes*. Cologne/Berlin: Athenäum, 1969.

Popper, Karl R. *The Logic of Scientific Discovery*. New York: Harper and Row, 1968.

Proust, Marcel. *In Search of Lost Time*, vol. VI: *Time Regained*, trans. Andreas Mayor and Terence Kilmartin, revised by D. J. Enright. New York: Modern Library, 1993.

Radnitzky, Gerard. *Contemporary Schools of Metascience*. New York: Humanities Press, 1970.

Reagan, Charles E. and David Stewart, eds. *The Philosophy of Paul Ricoeur: An Anthology of His Work*. Boston: Beacon Press/Toronto: Fitzhenry and Whiteside Limited, 1978.

Richards, I. A. *The Philosophy of Rhetoric*. New York: Oxford University Press, 1936.

Ricoeur, Paul. *The Conflict of Interpretations: Essays in Hermeneutics*, ed. Don Ihde. Evanston: Northwestern University Press, 1974.

———. "Le discours de l'action." In Dorian Tiffeneau, ed., *La Sémantique de l'action*. Paris: CNRS, 1977, 1–137.

——. *Fallible Man*, rev. trans. Charles A. Kelbley. New York: Fordham University Press, 1986.

——. *Freedom and Nature: The Voluntary and the Involuntary*, trans. Erzaim V. Kohák. Evanston: Northwestern University Press, 1966.

——. *Freud and Philosophy: An Essay on Interpretation*, trans. Denis Savage. New Haven: Yale University Press, 1970.

——. *From Text to Action: Essays in Hermeneutics II*, trans. Kathleen Blamey and John B. Thompson. Evanston: Northwestern University Press, 1991.

——. *Hermeneutics and the Human Sciences: Essays on Language, Action, and Interpretation*, ed. John B. Thompson. Cambridge: Cambridge University Press, 1981.

——. "I problem dell'ermeneutica," *Filosofia e Teologia* 2 (2006): 236–73.

——. "Intellectual Autobiography." In Lewis Edwin Hahn, ed., *The Philosophy of Paul Ricoeur*. Chicago: Open Court, 1995, 3–53.

——. *Memory, History, Forgetting*, trans. Kathleen Blamey and David Pellauer. Chicago: University of Chicago Press, 2004.

——. *Oneself as Another*, trans. Kathleen Blamey. Chicago: University of Chicago Press, 1992.

——. *The Rule of Metaphor: Multi-Disciplinary Studies in the Creation of Meaning in Language*, trans. Robert Czerny with Kathleen McLaughlin and John Costello, SJ. Toronto: University of Toronto Press, 1977.

——. "Self-Understanding and History," in T. Calvo Martinez and R. Avila Crespo, eds, *Paul Ricoeur: Los caminos de la interpretación*. Barcelona: Anthropos, 1991, 9–25.

——. *The Symbolism of Evil*, trans. Emerson Buchanan. New York: Harper and Row, 1967.

——. *Time and Narrative*, 3 vols, trans. Kathleen Blamey and David Pellauer. Chicago: University of Chicago Press, 1985–8.

Ritter, Joachim. *Metaphysik und Politik: Studien zu Aristoteles und Hegel*. Frankfurt: Suhrkamp, 1969.

——., ed. *Historisches Wörterbuch der Philosophie*. Basel: Schwabe, 1974.

Rorty, Richard, ed. *The Linguistic Turn: Recent Essays in Philosophical Method*. Chicago: University of Chicago Press, 1967.

Sartre, Jean-Paul. *Being and Nothingness: An Essay on Phenomenological Ontology*, trans. Hazel Barnes. New York: Philosophical Library, 1956.

Saussure, Ferdinand de. *Course in General Linguistics*, ed. Charles Bally and Albert Sechehaye in collaboration with Albert Riedlinger, trans. Wade Baskin. New York/London: McGraw-Hill 1966.

Seebohm, Thomas M. *Zur Kritik der hermeneutischen Vernuft*. Bonn: Bouvier, 1972.

Simon-Schäfer, Roland and Walter Ch. Zimmerli, eds. *Wissenschaftstheorie der Geisteswissenschaften*. Hamburg: Hoffman und Campe, 1975.

Stempel, W. D., ed. *Beiträge zur Textlinguistik*. Munich: Fink, 1971.

Stierle, Karl Heinz. *Text als Handlung: Perspektiven einer systematischen Literaturwissenschaft*. Munich: Fink, 1975.

Strachel, Günter. *Die neue Hermeneutik: Ein Überblick*. Munich: Kösel, 1968.

Strauss, Leo. *The Political Philosophy of Hobbes: Its Basis and Its Genesis*, trans. Elsa M. Sinclair. Chicago: University of Chicago Press, 1952.

Strawson, Peter. *Individuals: An Essay in Descriptive Metaphysics*. London: Methuen, 1959.

Taylor, Charles. *The Explanation of Behavior*. London: Routledge and Kegan Paul, 1964.

Theunissen, Michael. *Hegels Lehre vom absoluten Geist als theologsich-politischer Traktat*. Berlin: De Gruyter, 1970.

Tiffeneau, Dorian, ed. *La Sémantique de l'action*. Paris: CNRS, 1977.

Tugenhat, Ernst. *Der Wahrheitsbegriff bei Husserl und Heidegger*. Berlin: De Gruyter, 1967.

van Esbroeck, Michel. *Herméneutique, structuralisme et exégèse: Essai de logique herméneutique*. Paris: Desclée, 1968.

von Rad, Gerhard. *Old Testament Theology*, 2 vols, trans. D. M. G. Stalker. New York: Harper, 1962–5.

Wimsatt, W. K. *The Verbal Icon: Studies in the Meaning of Poetry*. Lexington: University of Kentucky Press, 1954.

Zimmermann, Jörg. *Wittgensteins sprachphilosophische Hermeneutik*. Frankfurt: Klostermann, 1975.

Index